The Silencing of Leonardo Boff

A Brief Chronology

April 16, 1927	Joseph Ratzinger born in Marktl am Inn, Bavaria
Dec. 14, 1938	Leonardo Boff born in Concordia, Brazil
June 29, 1951	Joseph Ratzinger ordained to the priesthood
Dec. 15, 1964	Leonardo Boff ordained to the priesthood
April 19, 1981	*Igreja: Carisma e poder* published by Editôra Vozes in Petrópolis, Brazil; English translation: *Church: Charism and Power* (New York: Crossroad, 1985).
May 15, 1984	Ratzinger's letter to Boff, summoning him to Rome
Sept. 2, 1984	Boff arrives in Rome
Sept. 3, 1984	"Instruction on Certain Aspects of the 'Theology of Liberation'" published
Sept. 7, 1984	Ratzinger-Boff colloquy
March 11, 1985	Ratzinger's Notification published
May 9, 1985	Boff's silencing imposed
March 13–15, 1986	Senior Brazilian bishops meet with Pope John Paul II in Rome
March 29, 1986	Boff's silencing lifted
April 5, 1986	"Instruction on Christian Freedom and Liberation" published
April 9, 1986	Letter of John Paul II to the Brazilian bishops, later delivered by Card. Bernadin Gantin

The Silencing of Leonardo Boff

The Vatican and the Future of World Christianity

HARVEY COX

COLLINS
FLAME

Collins Religious Publishing
8 Grafton Street, London W1X 3LA

Collins Dove
PO Box 316
Blackburn, Victoria 3130

Collins New Zealand
PO Box 1
Auckland

First published in the United States of America by Meyer—Stone
Books, a division of Meyer, Stone, and Company, Inc., in 1988

This edition first published in Great Britain by Collins Religious
Publishing, London, in 1989

ISBN 0 00 599196 X

© 1988 Harvey Cox

Printed and bound in Great Britain by William Collins Sons & Co.
Ltd, Glasgow

To
Nina and Nicholas

Contents

PART THREE: SILENCING

PART FOUR:
THE FUTURE OF WORLD CHRISTIANITY

Acknowledgments

Writing any book is always vastly enjoyable and terribly arduous. I raise here a grateful toast to some friends and colleagues, not only for the indispensable help they gave me while I was doing the research and the writing of this book, but also for the vast enjoyment and rich memories they made possible. My old friend Brady Tyson thoughtfully arranged a number of interviews for me in Brazil. Creuza Maciel introduced me to people I would never have met. Macio Moreiro Alves offered useful advice and made his lovely home in Petrópolis available to me. Pedro Ribeiro de Oliveira smilingly corrected some of my mistaken impressions. Brazilian bishops Adriano Hypolito and Mauro Morelli generously gave me their time — and counsel and coffee. Rui de Souza Josgrillberg, dean of the Methodist seminary in São Paulo, extended warmly welcoming hospitality. My former student Luisa Fernandes, also of São Paulo, guided me to some CEBs, and helped me understand them better. José Míguez Bonino and Jorge Pixley pushed me into seeing the Boff case in its larger perspective.

Margaret Studier, my secretary at Harvard Divinity School, not only typed this book in manuscript, but read it, commented on it constructively, rearranged it when necessary, and cheered me up when the going was slow. Robert Ellsberg and Sister Margaret Guider both read and offered useful suggestions on it at various stages. David Melton patiently worked over the footnotes. I am grateful to them all.

Although he may not agree with or appreciate all I have written here, I would also like to thank Cardinal Joseph Ratzinger, Prefect of the Sacred Congregation for the Doctrine of the Faith, for receiving me so cordially at his headquarters on the Largo Sant' Uffizio in Rome. I also learned much during the Roman phase of my research from Father Paul Patrick O'Leary, Director of Studies at the Dominican House of Studies on the Quattro Cantoni where, thanks to the hospitality of its residents, I also resided while in the Eternal City.

Finally I wish to thank Leonardo Boff, whose quiet courage and unbending resolution during his painful silencing taught me much about what it means to be a theologian who loves both the church and the truth.

PART ONE

The Controversy

When Rome Speaks...

On May 9, 1985, the Brazilian Franciscan theologian Leonardo Boff received an official notice from the Vatican that he was to begin immediately to observe an "obedient silence" for an unspecified period of time. The order was issued by Cardinal Joseph Ratzinger, who is prefect of the Sacred Congregation for the Doctrine of the Faith, an organ of the Roman curia that was known before the Second Vatican Council as the "Holy Office" and was once charged with the responsibility of conducting the Inquisition. The notice stated that the period of silence "would permit Friar Boff a time for serious reflection" but would require him to abstain completely from his duties as editor of the *Revista Eclesiástica Brasileira,* the most influential theological journal in Brazil, and to refrain from all his other activities as a writer and lecturer. The silencing was prompted by a heated discussion that had arisen about Boff's book *Church: Charism and Power,* in which he sharply criticized the way the hierarchy often exercises its authority in the Catholic church. The measure referred, of course, only to Boff himself, but since he is one of the most widely read proponents of the "theology of liberation" nearly everyone interpreted the silencing as a clear warning to that whole movement.

When Rome speaks, the old dictum says, the matter is closed (*Roma locuta, causa finita est*). But in this case quite the opposite happened. Rome's action closed nothing. Rather it opened up a worldwide controversy about Boff, liberation theology, and the long-range future of Christianity, one that continues into the present and shows no sign of abating.

This book is about that controversy and what we can learn from it about the future course of world Christianity. Sometimes nearly all the issues present in a crisis affecting a huge institution such as the Roman Catholic church can swirl into visibility in a single vivid incident. The part can reveal the whole. The silencing of Leonardo Boff provided just such an occasion. In recent years, Rome has criticized and disciplined other theologians. Edward Schillebeeckx and Hans Küng have both been summoned by the same Vatican congregation. Cardinal Ratzinger had earlier sent a highly critical communication to the Peruvian bishops about Boff's friend and mentor Father Gustavo Gutiérrez. Later he was to remove the American ethicist Charles Curran from his teaching post at the Catholic University of America and attempt to curtail the authority of Archbishop Raymond Hunthausen of Seattle. Still, though these cases all had certain similarities, the trial of Leonardo Boff revealed divisions that are deeper and more serious. It brought not just one man but a whole region of the Catholic church into conflict with Rome, and it raised questions not just about how the church should *act* but what the church *is* and what its message to the world should be.

Actually Boff knew about his silencing a few days before the official notice came. He had learned of it by way of a discreet personal letter prompted by Cardinal Ratzinger but sent by Boff's old friend Father John Vaughn, the minister general of his own religious order. Cardinal Ratzinger obviously wanted to handle the Boff case with considerable care for procedural rectitude. He was convinced that Boff's theology constituted a serious danger to the doctrine he is officially charged with safeguarding. But he is also sensitive to the unattractive history of the curial office he heads — at least of some of its episodes — and of the grim images of thumbscrews and racks its previous name, the "Holy Office," still calls up in many minds. He seemed determined to demonstrate that he intended to proceed both fairly and decisively, and that in keeping with the new mandate the Sacred Congregation had received at Vatican II, persuasion and positive teaching would replace the negative forms of discipline once used. The Boff case thus provided a kind of test of whether the new, more dialogical and fraternal methods would actually work.

On the same day the letter informing Boff about his silencing arrived in Brazil, the Vatican issued a succinct statement to the press in Rome. It stated that the Franciscan minister general had already communicated the terms of the "necessary measures" to the friar. Earlier rumors suggested the silence was to last one year,

but the announcement made clear that the official document fixed
no duration. It concluded with an assurance that the message
"had been received by the friar in a religious spirit." A few days
later, Boff himself wrote out a few sentences announcing that he
had accepted the decision of Rome. He then secluded himself in
the Franciscan Monastery of the Sacred Heart in the small city of
Petrópolis, located in the mountains just north of Rio de Janeiro;
Boff also lives and teaches in Petrópolis. He told friends that he
planned to abide by the silence and for the moment was not even
prepared to receive phone calls. But the friar's decision to accept
the Vatican's disciplining did not quell the debate. It pushed it
into a new stage.

Boff had already attracted considerable attention when the
same Sacred Congregation summoned him to Rome eight months
before his silencing, in September 1984, and then publicly condemned his views. Rome had also already severely criticized liberation theology itself in an "Instruction" issued while Boff was
in Rome. Now, as the announcement of the silencing was widely
reported in the secular press, he became something of an unwilling
celebrity. His broad face, gently curling hair, and thoughtful, direct
eyes behind goggle-style glasses appeared in newspapers and magazines all over the world. Letters, cards, and telegrams of support
arrived daily at the monastery. Many Brazilians looked upon the
Franciscan friar as a religious version of Pele, a champion of Latin
American religion and Brazilian national spirit against outside in-
truders. Ten Brazilian Catholic bishops took the highly unusual
step of publicly criticizing the Vatican's treatment of Boff. Various
Catholic groups and some Protestant religious bodies issued statements of support for Boff. Labor unions organized public demonstrations protesting the silencing. T-shirts and posters appeared
for sale in Brazil picturing Boff with his mouth gagged. Bishop
Pedro Casaldáliga, the Catholic bishop of São Félix do Araguaia
in the state of Mato Grosso, published a poem called "The Blessing
of St. Francis on Friar Leonardo Boff."

Boff himself declined to join any of the protests. He let his
supporters know that he appreciated what they were doing but
that he himself was not going to try to have the silence lifted,
even though he had no idea how long it would last. Months went
by. Catholic groups all over the world continued to complain to
Rome about what some called a rebirth of the Inquisition. The

Swiss weekly newspaper *Weltwoche* lamented that the late Pope John XXIII's promise — that dialogue and intellectual confrontation would now replace condemnations — "seemed gone with the wind." When Cardinal Ratzinger went to Paderborn, Germany, during the summer of 1985 to address 10,000 Catholics from several countries, he found himself picketed by youthful participants carrying placards denouncing the silencing. He chatted with them amiably and explained his position.

Gradually, however, the protests fell off. Fewer visitors found their way to the monastery. The number of letters dwindled. Boff became depressed. He told his sister he had begun to feel like a leper no one wanted to come near. When the leading Brazilian bishops were summoned to Rome in March 1986, his supporters were fearful that if his case came up at all, it would only result in the prolonging of the ban. The future of Boff and of the liberation theology he advocates looked anything but promising. Still, he maintained his silence.

Then in late March and early April of 1986 a series of unexpected events took place. Somehow the "summit" meeting of the Brazilian bishops with Pope John Paul II and the heads of the curial departments of the Vatican in March turned into a genuine exchange instead of a dressing down of the Latin Americans, who returned home hopeful and encouraged. A few days later, on March 29, Holy Saturday, Boff had just returned from saying mass in an outlying *favela* when he received a phone call in the monastery informing him that the silencing, which had lasted ten months, had been lifted. He told friends he had accepted the news "as an Easter present." Less than two weeks later the pope sent an unusually cordial letter to the Brazilian bishops, which was read at their annual meeting. In it he praised the theological renewal going on under their auspices as "a chance to renovate all of Catholic theology." A few days later, the Vatican officially issued a second statement on liberation theology entitled "Instruction on Christian Freedom and Liberation," which papal spokesmen said was intended to cast it in a more favorable light and to balance the earlier and highly critical document.

The flurry of events seemed perplexing. What had happened? Had Rome, or at least the pope, had a change of heart? Did the lifting of the ban on Leonardo Boff and the modulated tone of the new Instruction signal a different Vatican attitude toward liberation theology or a defeat for Cardinal Ratzinger and his curial allies? Was the Vatican simply trying to co-opt the language of liberation theology in order to rob it of its real impact? Had a secret deal been struck? Or was it, as one curial spokesman suggested, "an example of Vatican *Realpolitik*"? The responses of the liberation theologians themselves, both to the ending of the silence and to the new Vatican statement, did little to answer these queries. Boff himself praised the new document, telling the Milan daily *Corriere della Sera,* "After this, liberation theology gains a new dimension. The Vatican has given a universal significance to values that originally were those only of the Third World." But had Rome, really, done that? One aide to Cardinal Ratzinger thought Boff was slyly using this tactic to claim papal approval for liberation theology. "I'm not sure Father Boff read the document," he said, "because I don't see how it can be read to validate the positions of the liberation theologians." When he saw the new document, Father Gustavo Gutiérrez of Peru, the man who coined the term "liberation theology," dramatically announced that "this marks the end of an era. The debate is closed." But was it? Subsequent events, as we will see, strongly suggest that it was not. In fact, it had barely begun.

As the continuing saga of the Boff case unfolded, I thought back to the time I visited him in the Monastery of the Sacred Heart in July 1985, just a few weeks after his silencing began. He greeted me in baggy pants, a red flannel shirt, and a worn woolen sweater. He had begun to let his beard grow, a scraggly mixture of black and gray. He pluckily tried to joke about his "sabbatical year," but his humor seemed forced. Sometimes he appeared to withdraw from the conversation, his eyes remote behind the huge frames of his glasses. But then he would quickly catch himself and try to seem light-hearted again.

I was not the only visitor. I arrived just as fifteen or more theologians from all over Latin America were gathering in Petrópolis. It was a remarkable group. Juan Luis Segundo from Uruguay was there, the author of a multi-volume study of Jesus in historical and cultural perspective. So was Enrique Dussel, the gifted and energetic Argentine historian of Latin American Christianity presently living in Mexico. During a walk in the monastery garden I met Eduardo Hoornaert, the Brazilian church historian and chronicler of the base communities movement. Leonardo's brother Clodovis

Boff, a co-author of some of his books, was there. So was Hugo Ass-
mann, another Brazilian Catholic who now teaches at a Methodist
seminary. There were Protestant theologians too — Jorge Pixley,
the highly respected Baptist biblical scholar, who was on his way
from Mexico to a teaching post in Nicaragua; Elsa Tamez, the Old
Testament professor teaching in Costa Rica and one of the few
women liberation theologians; and José Míguez Bonino, an Argentine Methodist and former president of the World Council of
Churches. Sergio Torres of Chile presided over a meeting of the
group at which I was asked to bring greetings. Gustavo Gutiérrez
of Peru, the beloved "father" of the whole movement, drove in the
following day.

Ostensibly this galaxy of theological talent had arrived in the
tiny town of Petrópolis to discuss a common writing project, a kind
of multi-volume encyclopedia of liberation theology, each individual volume to be the fruit of cooperation between two or three
of the scholars. But there was obviously another purpose for the
gathering as well. They had all found their way to Petrópolis and
to the Franciscan Monastery of the Sacred Heart in order to be
with Leonardo. It was a demonstration of fraternal support, and
they were also curious. They wanted to hear what had happened
in Rome from Boff's own lips and to see how he was doing.

Boff had been assured by his superiors that the silencing was
not intended to stifle conversation with guests within the monastery, so one evening he spoke at some length informally and off the
record about the trip to Rome. He had gone, he said, expecting
to meet far more fairness and openness than he actually found.
The "colloquy" to which Ratzinger had invited him turned out
instead to be a full-scale interrogation, an ecclesial trial followed
by a verdict and, a few weeks later, by a sentence. Like many
a previous visitor to Rome, Boff told his colleagues he had come
to feel, sadly, there was something distinctly warped, maybe even
evil, about such a colossal concentration of ecclesial power. His description made me think of the well-known line in Martin Luther's
Appeal to the Ruling Class published in 1520: "The Romanists
themselves have coined the saying, 'The nearer Rome, the worse
the Christian....'" In any case, Leonardo's visit to the Eternal
City had only strengthened his opposition to the ways the Catholic church presently organizes and exercises its sacral power. But
unlike Luther, he had no desire whatever to break with the church.

He was, he said, determined to stay in it and with it — come what may.

Boff also said that during his often painful ordeal nothing had meant more to him than the support he had received from other Latin Americans, from his bishops, fellow priests, and from ordinary people. One Brazilian bishop, Boff confided, had even asked him — after he had returned from Rome — to read carefully through everything Cardinal Ratzinger had written, including his famous interview with Italian journalist Vittorio Messori, and then to draw up an indictment accusing him of heresy. Boff had turned down the request. Having been himself the object of such an inquiry he did not want to subject anyone else to it. All the theologians who heard this agreed with his decision, but one of them confessed to me later that he could not help finding something delicious about the prospect of the prefect of the Congregation for the Doctrine of the Faith himself being required to answer to charges of heterodoxy.

2

The Larger Sagas

I remembered my visit and the somewhat fanciful notion of indicting Cardinal Ratzinger for heresy when — back home on Easter Sunday 1986 — I heard the silence had been lifted and began to ponder what the Boff case really meant, not just in itself but for the future of Christianity. Then, as Boff faced new criticisms, investigations, and threats, I became increasingly convinced that Gustavo Gutiérrez's hopeful remark — that the debate was now over — was surely not correct. But a debate about what? To answer this question one must look not just at the ongoing story of Leonardo Boff, but also at the people, events and ideas that continue to play their parts in it. The case itself is far from over, and the issues it brings to world attention will continue to provoke controversy within the Catholic church and throughout world Christianity for many years to come. The Boff case contains within itself some even larger sagas. It includes:

1. The spectacular rise of liberation theology and the fierce opposition it has engendered;

2. the emergence of "Third World Christianity" and the consequent "de-Europeanization" of theology; and

3. the discomposure of currently dominant religious institutions in the face of energetic new grassroots spiritual movements.

It is these three often complex sub-plots — political, intellectual, and social — that have generated a debate that in fact is only now beginning.

1. The story of liberation theology is about how in less than twenty years, a quiet conversation among a few out-of-the-way Latin Americans became a worldwide theological movement. Boff is one of liberation theology's prominent figures, not as a seminal founder but as an eloquent interpreter and prolific writer. He has published thirty-five books on the subject and heads the religious division of the Brazilian publishing house Vozes, which prints the works of other liberation theologians. Hindering Boff's work was one obvious way for Rome to slow down the entire movement. But why does the Vatican seem to find Latin American liberation theology so threatening?

Newspaper and magazine accounts have made much of the accusation that liberation theologians allegedly make uncritical use of Marxist modes of analysis or that they "mix politics with religion." But hardly anyone who knows either the Vatican or the work of these theologians believes this is the issue. After all, even the pope himself sometimes speaks about "class" and "imperialism," and the role he plays — in Poland and elsewhere — can scarcely be described as entirely non-political. What then is the real cause of the Vatican's concern?

In their famous meeting at Medellín, Colombia, in 1968, the Latin American bishops proclaimed that the church should exercise a preferential option for the poor. Liberation theology is an expression of this preference. It is the attempt to interpret the Bible and Christianity from the perspective of the poor. It is in no sense a liberal or modernist theological deviation. Rather, it is a *method,* an effort to look at the life and message of Jesus through the eyes of those who have normally been excluded or ignored. From this angle of vision, liberation theologians believe they can uncover and correct distortions that have crept into Christianity over the centuries because theology has been almost exclusively the province of the privileged social stratas. To do this, they work closely with the burgeoning "Christian base communities" of Latin America. These are local groups of Catholics, most of whom are from the lowest tiers of society, whose study of the Bible has led them to become active in grassroots political movements. Thus liberation theology provides both an alternative to the top-down method of conventional academic and ecclesial theology as well as a source of guidance to the long-neglected people at the bottom. This results in a form of Christian theology that is biblical in its content, but is not easily subject either to hierarchical control or academic assessment. Naturally this makes both the curia and the academy apprehensive.

Critics of the liberation theology movement voice a variety of charges against it. Some claim it is insufficiently balanced, that it emphasizes the horizontal over vertical dimensions of faith. Others say it draws too heavily on the idea of class and class conflict in its understanding of the role of the poor, both in the Bible and in the contemporary world. Still others feel the liberation theologians are too wedded to particular sociological analyses, such as economic dependency theory, to explain the poverty in their countries.

Liberation theologians are aware of these charges. They admit their movement, though it draws on very old sources in the Bible and in the Christian tradition, is itself relatively new and needs time to mature. They welcome discussion, but they insist their work is in conformity with the gospel, and they deeply resent attempts to harass or censor them. The theologians, bishops, and other church leaders who rallied to the support of Boff did so not necessarily because they agreed with all his ideas. Many had differed with him in the past. They protested because they saw the silencing as a threat to everyone's right to think and write and as an unwelcome intrusion by Rome and Europe into a Latin American reality neither fully understood.

2. The second story concealed within *l'affaire Boff* is the rapid transformation of Christianity from a faith based principally in Europe and North America to a church whose members live mainly in Latin America, Asia, and Africa. Brazil now has the largest Catholic population in the world. According to the *Catholic Almanac*, about 480 million of the world's 825 million Catholics now live in Latin America, Africa, and Asia. This leaves the U.S.A. and Europe, including the U.S.S.R., with a minority of 338 million. (The remaining seven million are scattered around the rest of the globe.) A similar change is occurring among non-Catholics. The whole of Christianity is undergoing a rapid "de-Europeanization," a jarring demographic metamorphosis that is dismantling the thousand-year-old idea of "Christendom" and undermining a millennium-long style of theology. The church of Charlemagne and Innocent III, of Luther and Wesley and Pius XII, is already gone. In its place there is now appearing a Christian movement made up mostly of black and brown and yellow people, the majority of whom — if

current trends continue — will be forced to live their lives in the crowded, hungry megacities of the southern hemisphere. In nearly every Christian church in the world today whites are a shrinking minority.

Karl Rahner, the greatest European Catholic theologian of our time, once described the Second Vatican Council as "a leap to a world church." In his opinion, the shift from the Latin mass to the vernacular was in some ways the Council's most important achievement. Rahner wrote that it signaled unmistakably "the becoming of a world church where individual churches exist independently in their respective cultural spheres, inculturated, and no longer a European export." But Rahner also feared that the Roman curia might hinder the birth of a world church. It still had, in his words, "the mentality of a centralized bureaucracy which thinks it knows best what serves the kingdom of God and the salvation of souls throughout the world and in such decisions takes the mentality of Rome or Italy as its self-evident standard in a frighteningly naive way." [1]

Boff and his colleagues know about this centralizing mentality all too well. But it is easy to understand why some people think it is vital. Those who still believe the spiritual home of the church is Europe simply cannot accept what Eduardo Hoornaert calls the *desnortificação* ("de-northification") of Christian theology. The thought of it evokes fears of anarchy, collapse, and excess. African Catholics drum the mass and ask why the veneration of ancestors and polygamy are necessarily unchristian. By the ghats of the Ganges, Indian Christians meditate on the similarities between the Parusha and the Holy Spirit. Japanese Jesuits are working on a Zen version of the Ignatian Exercises. Where is the familiar uniformity, the comforting predictability that once made "Catholic" mean "same" and "Christian" mean "Western"?

Meanwhile, in Latin America, liberation theology, the first non-European theology ever to speak to the entire Christian world, has sprung forth out of the *favelas*. And Brazil is the center, both numerically and intellectually, of this growing movement. The attempt to quash Leonardo Boff was at the same time an effort to slow down or reverse a trend that, though it will probably not produce a Filipino or Nigerian or Brazilian pope in the near future, will inevitably change the church in profound ways. With the election of the cardinal archbishop of Cracow to the papacy, the Roman

Catholic church is no longer headed by an Italian. But Poland is still Europe, and the larger question is whether the Catholic church can transcend its "Europeanness," become a "world church," and still remain *one* church. This question also underlies the dispute between Ratzinger and Boff.

3. The third and perhaps the largest story inside the Boff episode is "the revolt of the base." It is reflected in the vexation of the leaders of the Christian church and of other religious institutions as they try to cope with one of the most unexpected reversals of the late twentieth century, the resurgence of religion.

Nothing seems to have turned out as anticipated. When the multiple eruptions of modernity, revolution, skepticism, and secularization staggered the soul of the nineteenth century, theologians responded in different ways. The Catholic church under the long papacy of Pius IX organized itself like an army, made the pope an infallible battle commander, and prepared for a protracted war of attrition. "Modernist" Catholics, who tried to come to terms with the contemporary world in some way other than with daggers drawn, were declared *personae non gratae*. Protestants, as usual, divided over the best way to manage. Liberal theologians from Schleiermacher to Tillich made imaginative attempts to speak to the modern world on its own terms, using the idiom of romanticism or existentialism. On the other side of town, conservative Protestants took a different tack. They endowed the Bible with what they called "literal inerrancy," an infallible authority it had never been granted before, and then clung to this "paper pope" as the landscape swayed around them.

But despite the tactical differences among these various religious parties concerning retreat or advance, negotiation or infiltration, or even surrender on the best possible terms, they all agreed on where the enemy lay. It lay in secularization in all its many guises — the modern attempt to expel God, as God had once expelled Adam. They saw modernity as a proud attempt to make the world over into a new Eden. It is true that the legions of secularization did not abolish religion completely. More often they tried to quarantine it to the heart of the individual, to the household hearth, to the "spiritual realm." But everyone knew modernity had the momentum. Nothing symbolized this better than the reduction of Catholicism's temporal sphere first from Christendom to the papal states, then to the 109 acres of the Vatican mini-state.

Then, in the latter half of the twentieth century, something quite unanticipated took place: religion itself was "born again." The post–World War II era witnessed a global revival and church leaders began to recognize that the enemy might not be secularization after all. Then, as the 1970s waned, the first Polish pope, having followed his immediate predecessor's example of refusing the papal tiara — the symbol of earthly power — nonetheless became the most influential pontiff since Innocent III, and possibly the most widely recognized and admired human being on earth. With John Paul II circling the globe and drawing millions of people to convocations, it was hard to claim that religion was still in irreversible decline. In the Protestant sphere, there were also signs of vitality. Pentecostalists, relying more on a direct emotional experience of the Spirit than on changeless precepts of Scripture, were multiplying so fast they promised to equal or surpass the more staid denominations in a few decades. American college and university students began enrolling in religion courses in unprecedented numbers. Even in western Europe, once dismissed as irreversibly "post-Christian," church attendance took a modest upturn in the 1980s. For the institutional churches, the dilemma now was no longer how to revive a comatose piety in an age of unbelief, but how to cope with fresh voices of faith that did not conform to the old patterns. Church leaders were faced not with a decline in spirituality but with a new outburst of religious energy. God was not, it seems, dead after all. But sometimes the God who was alive appeared to be more dangerous to the several religious establishments than the old secular foe they had come to know so well.

The threat Leonardo Boff poses to the Vatican is that he represents this grassroots religious energy boiling up from the bottom and the edges. A Franciscan priest, a theologian, a man of transparent religious courage and vigor, he is not the kind of antagonist Rome has become accustomed to dealing with. Boff and the movements of which he is a part — liberation theology, the Christianity of the non-European world, the faith of the disinherited — symbolize something vastly different from the rationalism Pius IX fought with the *Syllabus of Errors* or the skeptical scientism William Jennings Bryan attacked at the Scopes trial. The most fascinating question the Boff case raises is whether the established religious leaders and the dominant theological thinkers of today can shift gears for a time when, although secularization continues in many places, it no longer sets the cultural pace. John Paul II's recent encyclical *Dominus et Vivificatus* attacks atheism and materialism. But these were the heresies of the past. The most perplexing challenge Christianity will face in the decades ahead will not be these "isms" at all. Rather, Christianity now has to respond to the challenge posed by the rise of militant Islam, the revival of Shinto, the rebirth of fundamentalism in the United States and Israel, and a hundred other such movements. The next pope may fret more over spiritual zealotry than materialism and more over polytheism than atheism.

There are good reasons why religious leaders are apprehensive about these developments. Revival is never unambiguously good news for anyone. Religious feelings are often mixed with national, ethnic and racial loyalties. Fanaticism is always ugly, whether it wears the smile of the anti-religious tyrant or the frown of the devout bigot. But it would be naive to believe the managers of the different religious establishments are jittery about new spiritual movements just because of the harm they fear they may do to others. They are also worried about their own authority. Ecclesiastical bureaucracies and hierarchies are always upset by religious awakenings. Typically they try to discourage them, eliminate them, or channel them in directions that will allow the existing pillars of sacerdotal power to stand. For the canonical elites, Leonardo Boff represents not just an unmanageable galvanic wave but an uprising of the religious plebs — never a wholly welcome turn of events.

All these stories lie just below the surface of the dealings of the Sacred Congregation for the Doctrine of the Faith with one Franciscan friar. The trial of this theologian is also the trial of liberation theology. And the attack on liberation theology is the thrashing of Western Christianity as it watches its millennium-long hegemony drain. The trial also uncovers the understandable distress in the upper echelons of the world's great religious edifices as leaders see their authority threatened.

Perhaps the most obvious lesson of the Boff affair is that the present leaders of Christianity, including those of the Roman Catholic church, can no longer ignore the issues his case brings to the surface. They are questions that could once be kept safely within the province of professional theologians. But that is no longer true.

Boff was tried not just by the Congregation for the Doctrine of the Faith, but also by press releases and newspaper articles in the courtroom of world opinion. The arguments his case thrusts into the spotlight of world publicity cannot now be consigned again to the inner sanctum. Specifically, the case of Leonardo Boff produces *four key questions* that still remain unanswered:

1. What will the Catholic church do in the next decades about the powerful religious and intellectual movement represented by liberation theology that sees not just the heavenly salvation but the earthly liberation of the disinherited as the core of the gospel of Christ?

2. How will church leaders deal with a restless spiritual energy splashing up from the underside of society and threatening to erode traditional modes of ecclesial governance? It is their vitality and independence, not their so-called "political activism," that constitutes the real threat the thousands of "Christian base communities" all over Latin America pose for the hierarchy. How will the ecclesial elites respond?

3. How will Christian theology, inheritor of a two-thousand-year-old Western metaphysical tradition, come to terms with the rising "southern" tide that is reducing the old territory of Christendom to an island in a vast sea of cultural variety? Some believe the immensity of the change required is comparable only to the one Christianity underwent in the first hundred years of its life when it ceased to be a sect of Judaism and plunged into the world of Roman and Hellenistic culture.

4. How can the church respond to all this and still remain in some recognizable sense *one* church instead of a shambles of competing sects?

For awhile the Boff case appeared to have been a kind of Cuban missile crisis. Both sides found themselves shoved more quickly than they anticipated toward a confrontation neither really wanted. Having come eyeball to eyeball, both discreetly backed away. But now, as the case drags on, everyone secretly recognizes that all the perplexing and pervasive issues that brought the adversaries to the brink are still there. One day, one way or another, these questions will have to be faced.

At one level, perhaps the most profound one, these are theological issues. Theology is said to be thinking about God. But, as most theologians agree, since the Mystery of God itself remains inexpressible, theology must be about people, their faith, and the experiences and ideas they have of God and the world. Theology is not, or should not be, an esoteric discipline reserved for specialists. Hence, we will begin with the Boff story itself and introduce the main actors. Then we will trace the ideas that impelled them, and conclude with some suggestions about how the logic of the story can help all the disagreeing parties move beyond confrontation and toward conversation.

PART   TWO

The Friar and the Prefect

3

The Summons

In early 1981, the Vozes publishing house in Brazil published a book in Portuguese by Leonardo Boff entitled *Igreja: Carisma e Poder* (Church: Charism and Power). Two other presses, Sal Terrae in Santander, Spain, and Borla in Rome, brought it out in Spanish and Italian at the same time. Boff, who is a widely read theologian, hoped of course that the volume would find an audience, but he was not unduly optimistic. After all, the book was a potpourri of disparate writings with only a minimal unifying theme. Some parts were transcriptions of talks he had given at conferences and discussion groups. Others had already appeared in religious magazines. The slender thread that ties the book loosely together is its thesis that both the institutional and the spiritual elements in the church are essential, but — since power has so often stifled spirit — the two need to be brought into more equilibrium. True, a couple of essays describe this stifling in some detail. But the main thrust of the book is that the dynamic and the structural aspects of the church could, with care, be harmonized. By and large, the tone is positive and hopeful. Still, neither the title nor the subject matter seemed to invite widespread public debate. Collections of essays on ecclesiology rarely make the bestseller lists.

Almost immediately, however, at first mainly among theologians, this book provoked an unusual amount of discussion, both positive and negative. Both Boff's critics and his supporters agreed on one thing at least: that he had caused the stir by applying the insights of liberation theology — previously utilized mainly to address the ills of secular society — to the church itself. For example, he had raised questions about how the church could hope to be a credible advocate of human rights in the world when it denies some of these rights within itself. Due process was an example cited.

21

The critics took sharp issue with his description of the church's governance in terms usually reserved for analyzing worldly injustice. Some critics were particularly incensed that in one essay he applied the term "system of religious production," which sounds like a term from economics, to the hierarchy. They also questioned his use of the words "symbolic violence" to refer to the methods the church sometimes uses — such as silencing and excommunications — to discourage dissent. (In view of what was to happen to Boff within a few years of the publication of the book, however, his observations on this last point now seem almost prescient.)

One of Boff's earliest critics was his former theological teacher, Bonaventura Kloppenburg, who soon after the book appeared was named bishop of the Brazilian city of Salvador. Kloppenburg published his review first in the spring of 1982 in a journal called *Communio,* which was organized in 1975 as a conservative counterweight to another Catholic theological journal called *Concilium.* *Concilium* had appeared immediately after the Second Vatican Council, and it quickly became the organ of those theologians — including the Dutch Edward Schillebeeckx, the Swiss Hans Küng, and the Brazilian Leonardo Boff — who had come into their own during the Council and who were designated, mainly by their critics, as "the progressives."

Even before Kloppenburg's criticism appeared, some conservative members of the Brazilian hierarchy had begun to look with disfavor at Boff's work. The newly organized archdiocesan Commission for the Doctrine of the Faith of Rio de Janeiro, the local equivalent of the office in Rome which was later to silence Boff, made the investigation of the book its first major project. Its president, Bishop Karl Joseph Romer, authorized Father Urbano Zilles to write a review, which was published in the *Boletim da Revista do Clero* in February 1982. It stated that Boff "...begins with the assumption that the institutional church as it now exists has nothing to do with the Gospel," and that Boff thought most of the church's present teaching was nothing but deception and illusion, that the task of theology was to "unmask and demystify it."[1]

Boff sharply disagreed with Father Zilles's reading of his book and responded in the April edition of the same *Boletim.* The editors included Zilles's rejoinder to Boff's response in the same issue. When Boff in turn asked to reply to this rejoinder, they declined, so he sent it instead to a journal called *Grande Sinal,* which published it along with yet another answer, this time by a Father Estevo Bettancourt, who is a member of the same Rio de Janeiro Archdiocesan Commission for the Doctrine of the Faith.

By now, most readers of these journals were growing tired of the debate, and Boff himself for the most part considered it over. It came as a surprise to Boff, therefore, when Kloppenburg's original criticism from *Communio* was reprinted with considerable fanfare in the Sunday edition of the widely read Rio de Janeiro secular newspaper *Jornal do Brasil* in June 1982, thus exposing the broader public to what had been a protracted squabble among theologians. From then on, the Boff case was no longer just an intra-church argument. It became an event the media followed with growing attention. The trial had begun.

Meanwhile, in February 1982, Boff, who knew his critics had already complained to the Vatican about him, took the precaution of mailing to the Congregation for the Doctrine of the Faith in Rome copies of Zilles's unfavorable review and of his reply. He says he did so merely as a matter of courtesy, but the fact that he appears to have initiated this contact allowed some of his critics to claim later on that, in effect, he had asked for trouble. In any case, on April 14, 1982, he received a letter from Cardinal Joseph Ratzinger, the prefect of that congregation, informing him that the congregation had received his materials and asking him to respond also to the criticisms Kloppenburg had published in *Communio*. Boff wrote a reply, sent it, and also published it in the June 1982 issue of *Revista Eclesiástica Brasileira*. In the same issue, the journal also published a long summary of the whole debate by Father Carlos Palacio, S.J. The publication of this summary appeared to Boff another reason to consider the matter closed and to move on to other tasks. In fact, for nearly two years, nothing more happened.

The matter, however, was far from closed. In May 1984, three years after his book first appeared, Boff received a six-page letter delivered to him through Friar John Vaughn, the minister general of the Franciscans, from Cardinal Ratzinger. In it, the cardinal listed several criticisms and stated that many of the positions set forth in the book "did not merit acceptance." Ratzinger's letter touched on some very delicate questions, such as Boff's theological method, his statement on the structure of the church, the concepts of dogma and revelation he propounds, and his description of the exercise of sacral power. In the closing paragraph he offered Boff the opportunity for a "colloquy" in Rome within the next couple of months. Finally, the cardinal noted that "in view of the influence the book in question has had on the faithful," he intended to make his letter to Boff public. While delivering the letter to Boff, Father Vaughn also passed on a verbal message in which Cardinal Ratzinger expressed his hope that the theologian would "receive the observations favorably and would give a prompt response" to the matter of the colloquy.

Boff wrote back immediately that he would accept the colloquy and asked more about its exact nature. Was it to be an official juridical hearing under the provisions of canon law? Or was something else envisioned? He inquired if the colloquy could be held with the cooperation of the Brazilian Bishops' Commission on Doctrine, whose president is Cardinal Aloísio Lorscheider, and whether it could possibly take place in Brazil. He asked further that, if it were not possible for the colloquy to be held in Brazil, could it be scheduled a little later.

On June 16, Cardinal Ratzinger responded that the colloquy would take place just between the two of them, though in the presence of a third person selected by Ratzinger. It would be held in Rome, since there was no provision in canon law either for such a colloquy to take place elsewhere, or in conjunction with the Brazilian doctrinal commission. He also made clear that although the invitation was to a colloquy, and not to an interrogation, indeed the meeting would still have an official character. He set the date tentatively for the 7th or 8th of September 1984, indicating that some slight postponement might be possible. He repeated his intention to publish his earlier six-page letter of objections to Boff's book.

Boff continued to try to have the colloquy take place in Brazil. On August 8, 1984, he wrote Ratzinger suggesting that a Brazilian meeting would be more in keeping with the Second Vatican Council's spirit of "collegiality" (sharing authority with the bishops) and of "subsidiarity" (doing everything possible at lower rather than higher levels). In this letter, Boff also asked the identity of the other person who would participate in the colloquy, requested access to the information they had assembled about him, inquired what language they would speak, and asked who would pay for the flight to Rome. In closing, Boff asked that Ratzinger's six-page letter not be published before the colloquy, since he believed it contained errors in its citations, both from his own book and from the pope. He suggested to the cardinal that releasing the letter in its present form might cast doubt on the seriousness of the discussion.

Convinced now that he would in fact be going to Rome, Boff met with several of the Brazilian bishops to ask their advice. During these conversations he learned that Bishop José Ivo Lorscheiter, president of the 400-member Brazilian bishops' conference, planned to be in Rome anyway in early September. Lorscheiter offered to see if it could be arranged for him to accompany Boff to the colloquy, along with his colleague Cardinal Aloísio Lorscheider, the president of the Brazilian Bishops' Commission on Doctrine. (Ivo Lorscheiter and Aloísio Lorscheider are sometimes confused with one another because their names sound nearly the same, although they are spelled differently.) Further, the cardinal archbishop of São Paulo, Dom Paulo Evaristo Arns, who had tentative plans to pass through Rome in the late summer on his way back from a trip to Poland and Germany, also indicated his interest in taking part in the colloquy. Boff was obviously gratified by the willingness of these leaders of the Brazilian hierarchy, all of whom he considered sympathetic, to appear in Rome with him. He then waited for further word from the Vatican. Finally, on August 30, 1984, the apostolic nuncio in Brazil, Father Carlo Furno, informed Boff that the colloquy had been scheduled for September 8, 1984, and that it would proceed in whatever language seemed most convenient to the participants. The Vatican would pay for the ticket.

Boff arrived in Rome on September 2, 1984. By now his case had become something of a *cause célèbre*. At the airport, crowds of journalists jostled him while asking questions. Boff looked around anxiously and finally spotted his brother, Father Clodovis Boff, who was already in Rome to pursue courses at the Marianum, and his sister Lina Boff, who had been working in Rome for five years. (Shortly after he welcomed his brother to Rome, Clodovis Boff learned that he would not be able to pursue his studies because the Cardinal of Rio de Janeiro, Eugenio Sales, a strong critic of the Boff brothers, had forbidden him to do so.)

Boff wanted to get away from the airport quickly, but he sensed that he would have to say something to the journalists. He decided to be brief. "I am in Rome," he told them, "not as a pilgrim, not as a tourist, and not as a participant in some kind of theological congress. I have been summoned to Rome by the prefect of the Sacred Congregation for the Doctrine of the Faith. I intend to respond to the questions he asks me, not to those of journalists. I am in the diocese of the pope. Out of respect for him, I intend to speak only within the Sacred Congregation." With that he climbed into the car his sister had driven to the airport with Clodovis and left.

Boff passed his time in Rome almost entirely within the walls of the Franciscan headquarters (called the "General Curia") near the Vatican. From his window, he could look out on the dome of St. Peter's Basilica. From the day after his arrival until his meeting with Cardinal Ratzinger five days later, he read and studied to prepare himself for the questions the Cardinal had raised about his book. Sometimes he chatted with the other Franciscans who were living in the same quarters and tried out the ideas he had jotted down in a sixty-seven-page manuscript, brought with him from Brazil, to respond to Ratzinger's six-page letter. But mostly he rested, prayed, and waited.

4

David and Goliath

From the earliest days of Boff's trouble with Rome, the world press depicted it as an uneven battle. It was David and Goliath all over again. Boff was cast as the boy with the slingshot, and Ratzinger seemed the logical heavy to play the Philistine titan. In one sense the prefect had himself contributed to the morality play scenario by singling Boff out. But the confrontation went far beyond a contest of personalities. Neither did it square with its depiction in the media as a competition between an innovative young liberal who wanted to push ahead and a reactionary standpatter who was using his power to roll the church back. The issues were far more nuanced, more serious, and more divisive.

To start with, Boff is no David, and Ratzinger is anything but a Philistine. Boff, after all, is an immensely productive writer and highly influential publicist. When he landed at the Rome airport in September 1985 for his "colloquy" with Ratzinger, Boff, at the age of forty-six, was already head of the religion section of Vozes, one of the largest publishing houses in Brazil. He was also the editor of the *Revista Eclesiástica Brasileira,* by far the most widely read journal of pastoral theology in the largest Catholic country on earth. He has numerous friends and colleagues both in Latin America and in the entire liberation theology movement worldwide. He is an amazingly prolific writer with thirty-five titles and numberless articles and reviews to his credit. Furthermore, Boff's books are very widely read. Just before he returned to Brazil from his youthful period of study in Europe, Boff told his fellow student Ludovico Gramus, "When I get back to Brazil I am going to write the kind of theology people can read the way they read a newspaper." This is just what he did, and even his most determined antagonists admit he writes with clarity and verve. This engaging style, together with the important ideas he discusses, have gained him a large audience. At the publishing house that handles his books, Boff is affectionately known as "the Jorge Amado of faith." This is an exaggeration, of course. Since 1975, the great Brazilian novelist Amado has sold five million copies of his various novels. Still, the sale of Boff's books is now approaching half a million. His overall bestseller, *Jesus Christ, Liberator,* has been translated into ten languages. In the critical battle of ideas in which he has been so energetically engaged for many years now, these statistics add up to more than just a few pebbles or a slingshot.[1]

Leonardo Boff was born in 1938 in the Brazilian city of Concordia in Santa Catarina state, the son of a primary school teacher who had to work hard to support his eleven children. The brothers and sisters have remained unusually close throughout their adult lives. Friends and family report that little Genesio (which was what Boff was called until he took the name "Leonardo" at his ordination, since there was no St. Genesio on the list of saints) seemed to have been born for the priesthood. He never considered anything else very seriously, entered the minor seminary at ten, and seems never to have regretted it. A friend once remarked that if someday priests are allowed to marry, he is sure Leonardo will remain celibate. His friends agree that he is the kind of person who, having committed himself to a course of action, is hard to dissuade. Indeed, during the long altercation he eventually had with Rome, his ecclesiastical superiors found out how determined a person he could be.

Boff attended the major seminary in Petrópolis, where he now teaches, and became the favorite pupil of Father Bonaventura Kloppenburg, who has since become one of his severest critics. He was ordained to the priesthood as a Franciscan in 1964, became Kloppenburg's secretary for a time, then completed his formal education in Munich, where in 1971 he submitted his doctoral dissertation to then-professor Joseph Ratzinger, the same man who as prefect of the Sacred Congregation for the Doctrine of the Faith would eventually become his principal antagonist. The thesis was entitled "The Church as Sacrament in the Horizon of World Experience" and was judged by his professors to be not only acceptable, but brilliant and unusually promising. Back in Brazil, "Neio" (short for "Genesio" and the name by which his closest friends and family still call him) immediately plunged into the whirl of teaching, writing, and pastoral work that still engages him. He is the most widely read and perhaps the most influential liberation theologian in the world today.

If Boff is no biblical David, Ratzinger is hardly a Philistine, at least in the modern metaphorical sense of "one who looks down on or is smugly indifferent to culture or aesthetic refinement."[2] His most vociferous critics are the first to concede that the cardinal-prefect possesses one of the keenest theological minds in the curia today. Known first as one of the brilliant young progressives of the Second Vatican Council, he has also published over thirty books, has taught theology in some of the leading universities of Germany, and has won a deserved reputation for his intellectual sure-footedness. He is without any doubt the most broadly educated and scholarly person ever to hold the post some call the "chief gendarme of orthodoxy," the prefect of the office in the Vatican curia charged with maintaining the integrity of doctrine in the Roman Catholic church.

Boff and Ratzinger are so much alike and yet so different. Their confrontation in Rome was, however, no mere *coincidentia oppositorum*. Rather it brought together two committed and confident men who share some passionate concerns but who differ on precisely the issues they feel so strongly about. They also share some remarkably parallel life circumstances. For example, both have brothers who also became priests. Boff's brother Clodovis, however, continues to work closely with him while Ratzinger and his brother Georg have gone somewhat separate ways. The two Ratzinger bothers were ordained to the priesthood together on the same day, June 29, 1951, by Cardinal Archbishop Michael von Faulhaber, in the Freising Cathedral. A photo album published later in Munich in 1977, when Ratzinger himself became a cardinal, includes a fetching picture of the two young men, hands stretched out, bestowing their first priestly blessings at their *Primiz*. Both Joseph and Georg are clad in intricate baroque surplices and elaborate lace stoles.

But there are already hints of the different directions they were to take. Georg, who became a parish priest, is smiling broadly and looking toward the congregation. Joseph appears deeply serious and is gazing down. Joseph's hands are spread wider. Shortly after the picture was taken, Joseph left his pastoral duties to begin his spectacular ascent: a noted scholar; a *peritus* at Vatican II; a

founder of *Concilium,* the organ of the postconciliar "progressives";
a respected professor of theology at Münster, Tübingen, and Regensburg; an editor of *Communio,* the "rival" of *Concilium;* the
bishop of Munich; and now the cardinal-prefect of the Congregation for the Doctrine of the Faith. Georg is now a choirmaster in
Regensburg.

Like Boff, Ratzinger has never been viewed as one of the most
seminal or original representatives of his school of theology. But
the Bavarian Ratzinger, like the Brazilian Boff, has been astonish-
ingly productive. By the time he left Munich for Rome in 1982, he
had published thirty books. Like Boff, he has also written about a
variety of subjects, beginning in 1953 with the book for which he
was awarded his degree from Munich, a study of St. Augustine's
doctrine of the church. His experience with the Vatican Council
provided material for no less than four books between 1963 and
1966. But, like Boff, he takes a special pleasure in writing "pastoral" books, ones ordinary lay people might find edifying. He has
written such tracts on the significance of Holy Week, on the question of God, and on the significance of Mary. When one remembers
that Boff has also written semi-popular works on the meaning of
Christ's passion (*Passion of Christ — Passion of the World*)[3] and
on Mary (*The Maternal Face of God*),[4] it is evident that the two
men have remarkably convergent interests. They even share a common love for the great thirteenth-century Franciscan theologian St.
Bonaventure, about whom Ratzinger wrote a book in 1957, which
won him wide recognition. Both, however, have a practical turn
of mind, and each has consistently shown that his most enduring
fascination is with the question of the nature of the church and its
task in the world. It was both their common interest and their
deep differences about this issue — what the church should be and
what it should be doing — that eventually propelled them into conflict with each other and brought the friar to the prefect's office in
September 1984.

Let us return now to the friar and to the intellectual and personal trajectory that brought him from Brazil to Rome. The
church adjacent to the Franciscan monastery of the Sacred Heart
in Petrópolis stands on a noisy street lined with barber shops,
tiny restaurants, and strong-smelling grocery stores. Buses, cars
with faulty exhaust pipes, and assorted delivery trucks keep the
noise level several decibels above what one normally expects in

a monastery precinct. The congregation attending the evening mass on the day I visited was dressed poorly and was predominantly black. After the benediction, most of them, including a large number of young children, lined up two abreast all around the outer aisles and filed slowly past a side door to a room behind the altar area where an elderly monk in a brown robe presided over the distribution of food packages. Waiting, some patiently and some fidgeting, these parishioners, clothed in rubber beach sandals, T-shirts, torn shorts, and frayed print dresses, sketched a visual counterpoint to the stations of the cross and the plaster-of-Paris pietà they were shuffling past. Franciscans, like many other Christians, have frequently lost the close contact with the humble people Jesus and Francis sought out. But the monks in this monastery have not. Both the Poverello from Assisi and the prophet from Nazareth would have felt quite at home.

The monastery itself stands just a few steps from the church. It fronts on a miniature parking lot where children scream and chase each other amidst the Volkswagens, while weary mothers with bags of food wait for the bus. It is a raucous and sometimes ear-splitting scene. But just inside the monastery's huge green wooden doors the atmosphere changes. The visitor enters through a delicate garden, its air sweetened by the smell of eucalyptus and freshly watered flower beds. At the center stands a life-sized statue of St. Francis with the wolf of Gubbio nuzzling his hand. One has only to savor these streets and to enter the portal of the place Boff chose to serve out his silence to realize that his being a Franciscan is hugely important to this man.

The more I perused his books and articles, and the longer I observed his surroundings, the clearer it became to me that for Boff liberation theology is not some novel departure or trendy innovation. Rather it signifies a continuation of the spirit of St. Francis in the contemporary church. His friends and colleagues recognize this too. This may be why, just after the silencing, Bishop Pedro Casaldáliga of São Félix do Araguaia, who is a Claretian, composed his poem "The Blessing of St. Francis on Friar Leonardo Boff," which was widely published in Brazil. "What would my compadre St. Francis say to his son Leonardo Boff," asked the bishop, "in this the hour of his provocation?" His answer to his own question runs as follows:

Brother Leonardo,
theologian of liberating grace
by the design of God:
Even though the way the Vatican
treats brothers in the faith
does not seem to conform
to the Gospel of freedom,
you, Brother Leonardo,
as one who remembered and follows
our Lord and Liberator
who became obedient
unto death, even death on the cross,
you too should obey
with the good humor of a
little brother of the Kingdom.
Be now for some days
a theologian of silence.
Partake of the profound mystery
of the poor,
who have no voice anyway
either in the church or in society.

Casaldáliga does not counsel protest or rebellion. Rather, he ad-
vises Boff that even though the silencing may be unjust, it could
conceal a blessing. In the rush of his busy life as scholar and editor,
the silencing might provide Boff an opportunity to listen anew to

the outcry of the poor
which issues forth
from this continent of death
and of hope.
And the new song which breaks forth
from fields and cities
and from the countryside.

Chosen prophet
of such luminous words,
be, for a little while, a silent prophet
and your heart will feel
a perfect joy.[5]

Throughout Boff's ordeal, many of the church leaders who supported him most constantly — Cardinal Arns, Cardinal Lorscheider, Bishop Adriano Hypolito of Rio de Janeiro, Father Vaughn — were Franciscans. Boff's commitment to follow the saint of Assisi is the rosetta stone for anyone trying to understand his mind and spirit.

5

Francis and Bonaventure

In 1981, Boff wrote an exquisite little book about St. Francis.[1] In it, he emphasized the simplicity of the saint as a model for a world glutted by consumption and accumulation. He also pointed out that for our age of such vast inequity, St. Francis's personal love for the poor, which grew into his identification with the life of "the poor Christ," has a particularly exemplary relevance. And he emphasized how much St. Francis's affection for the grass and the birds has to tell us in a period of ecological spoliation. The son of a well-off family, Francis had decided to cast aside his costly raiment and wear the roughest clothing of his time, cinched at the waist not with a leather belt but with a common cord of hemp: thus "naked to follow the naked Christ." But contrary to many of the prevailing theologies of the day, Francis did not consider natural beauty a distraction from God. For him it was a luminous medium through which the divine and the human could meet. Some cultural historians even hold that by inspiring Giotto, many of whose paintings depict the saint's life, Francis himself became a forerunner of that affirmation of the terrestrial world that blossomed later in the Renaissance. Boff is also a world-affirmer. One can sense in his general bearing as well as in the tone of his writing a kind of hopefulness and a continuous confidence in the underlying goodness both of the created world and of human cultural activity. In reading Boff one catches a glimpse of his belief that the earth — despite the agony he sees around him all the time — is not just a veil of tears but a womb filled with life.

Another element in the spirituality of St. Francis that seems even more pertinent to Boff is the saint's bold insistence that lay people and not just clergy were an integral part of the community of faith. In St. Francis' own time, the priests and bishops and nuns and monks were generally viewed as constituting "the church." Lay people were expected to be passive and deferential recipients of the sacraments, the teachings, and the discipline meted out by the hierarchy, and the beneficiaries of the intercessory prayers of the cloistered monks and nuns. Religious movements initiated by the laity were discouraged and lay leadership forbidden.

St. Francis challenged this whole schema. He did something the liberation theologians call "ecclesiogenesis": he created a new form of church life. He organized a religious fraternity of ordinary people who wanted to follow Jesus in the world and not in a monastery. This was a radical departure. Anyone who chose to do so could participate without ordination or theological training and — at least in its early years — without the extended period of novitiate required by the monasteries. Thus Francis, who was not a priest himself, contributed to the growing importance of the laity within the "people of God," an emphasis which, many centuries later, became one of the principal advances of the Second Vatican Council. Boff constantly returns to the theme of lay participation, and this continues to be one of the sore spots between him and his critics today.

The Poverello of Assisi went even further. First he encouraged St. Clare (1194–1253) to found a comparable movement for women, also based on the "spirit of poverty." Then he took another step. He created the Order of Penitents, later called the "Third Order Secular," which permitted married laymen to become Franciscans while continuing to live as businessmen, husbands, soldiers, and political leaders — still observing the basic Franciscan values.

Early on, Francis had brought his plans to the pope and offered to place his movement, which he called the Order of Friars Minor, under papal authority — at least officially. Fortunately for Francis, the pope at the time was Innocent III, perhaps the shrewdest ecclesiastical statesman ever to occupy the papal throne. Previous popes had dealt severely with such groups and had normally forbidden lay people to preach or teach. But Innocent III had shown more flexibility than his predecessors even before Francis appeared. He had already welcomed under papal protection a group which, having broken off from the heretical Waldensians, called themselves the "Poor Catholics." The pope gave them permission to preach in public so long as they concentrated on moral exhortation and did not touch on doctrine. Innocent III was sagacious. He saw that

in the Franciscan movement, and in Francis himself, he was faced
with a genuine spiritual upsurge that he could manage better if he
approved it than if he banned it.

Giotto's well-known painting of St. Francis and Innocent III has
preserved for posterity the critical moment when the friar and the
pope met. But what the painting does not show is that the religious
vision Francis represented is ultimately irreconcilable with the hierarchical order Innocent III devoted his pontificate to building
and defending. Already by the time Giotto was painting, tensions
had broken out between the papacy and the Franciscans. Indeed
one could argue that the painting was an inspired piece of propa-
ganda whose purpose was to disguise these difficulties and co-opt
the Franciscan energy for papal purposes. In any case, the contradictions have never disappeared. The trial of Leonardo Boff may
be only the latest chapter in a very long saga.

It took another painting, however, to enable me to understand
how Boff's own brand of Franciscan spirituality informs his understanding of theology. One room in the library of the Monastery of
the Sacred Heart is lined with antique books that are so old and
so rarely used by the friars that they now serve a kind of genteel
decorative function. The floor is covered by a worn wine-colored
carpet, and the monks use the space between the polished shelves of
gold-tooled morocco and buckram volumes for entertaining guests,
sipping beer, and holding informal receptions. In this venerable
old chamber on a cool July evening in 1985, the theologians who
had come from far and wide to visit Brother Leonardo gathered
to say farewell. It was noisy for a library, but the air had a feeling Brazilians describe with the untranslatable Portuguese word
saudade: the term conveys something of the fine mixture of feelings Shakespeare calls forth when he speaks of the "sweet sorrow"
of parting. We all knew we were leaving and that a new and possibly more painful phase of Leonardo's silence would begin when
we were gone.

After I'd said my own good-bye, someone suggested taking a
picture. Boff agreed. Then, glancing around the wall of the room,
he pointed to a large oil painting and suggested we pose together
in front of it. On this particular canvas, St. Bonaventure (1221–
1274), the most celebrated of all Franciscan theologians, is seated,
quill in hand, at a writing desk strewn with folios and foolscap.
A glowing apparition of the Blessed Virgin hovers in the upper

right-hand corner of the picture, sending an incandescent shaft, presumably of inspiration, directly onto the page in front of the theologian. "He's writing," Boff explained, "about the Immaculate Conception."

I thought Boff's suggestion for the location of the snapshot was appropriate. So we utilized the mystery of the flashbulb to bring into our twosome not St. Francis himself but St. Bonaventure: not the charismatic founder of the order but its chief theologian, the "Seraphic Doctor," the man who is sometimes called the "second founder" of the Order of Friars Minor. St. Bonaventure is the disciple who tried to follow the Poverello with his head as well as with his heart. In his public statement after the Notification, Boff referred to himself as "a Christian, a Franciscan, and a theologian." He is a friar, but he is also a Franciscan *theologian* who has always loved and admired Bonaventure. I believe that knowing something about Bonaventure helps us know something important about Boff, or at least about the kind of person Boff would like to be.

Bonaventure was born near Viterbo, Italy, and entered the heady world of the University of Paris at the age of eighteen, receiving the Master of Arts degree in 1243 at the age of twenty-six. Upon graduation, he immediately joined the Franciscans and began to teach at their own school near Paris. His biographers describe him as an attractive, bright, and spiritually serious young man who loved St. Francis (whom he later claimed had interceded for him when he had been deathly ill as a child) but who was just too curious and intellectually inclined to accept the saint's suspicion of books and learning.

This ambivalence about the life of the mind caused the young Bonaventure much inner disquietude. I think Boff, as a teacher of theological students, also appreciates the predicament. Head versus heart: it is a common conflict among such students even today. Many feel their faith intensely or at least believe their own personal religious quest is something terribly important. But they also have lively, inquisitive minds, and they are sometimes afraid that too much critical analysis could spoil it all. The young Bonaventure seems to have resolved the perplexity by transforming learning itself into an expression of praise. It is a solution the long tradition of Jewish study of Torah has nourished for centuries. It is also the way Leonardo Boff seems to have combined his buoyant Franciscan spirituality with his restless, searching mind.

Later Bonaventure, like Boff, began to teach at a Franciscan school of theology and to write books. Just as Boff must constantly answer the foes of liberation theology, Bonaventure had to answer the critics of the Franciscans who complained that no one could possibly combine the rigors of life as a mendicant with the rigors of being a scholar. This criticism is comparable to the one often leveled at liberation theologians today by their more academically oriented colleagues who imply that no one can be an activist and a theologian at the same time. Bonaventure firmly insisted that one could — and demonstrated it in his own career. So does Boff. Bonaventure continued to teach and write and administer until he left the school in 1257 upon being elected "minister general," the title given the head of the Franciscan order. Boff writes, teaches, edits, administers Vozes, and still manages to travel widely in Brazil and other countries.

As minister general, Bonaventure went on writing even though he had to cover hundreds of miles to visit the various outposts of his growing and often discordant new order. In fact, his masterpiece, *Journey into the Mind to God,* was written during this tumultuous period, and since he was always on the road, the metaphor of the journey is hardly accidental. Bonaventure was an ardent advocate of reconciliation between factions within the church and between Eastern and Western Christianity. He actually died at a council devoted to such unity efforts in 1274.

Boff is also a peacemaker. Although he is sometimes pictured by his critics as combative (and when he needs to be, he is), one is struck in reading his books by the strenuous effort he makes to appreciate the views of those with whom he disagrees. There is every reason to believe that he went to Rome quite willingly, and honestly expected to find some common ground with his former teacher Cardinal Ratzinger and maybe even to effect some reconciliation.

For me, Bonaventure had been an attractive figure long before Leonardo Boff posed the two of us under his portrait. My own theological teacher, Paul Tillich, had always described himself as standing within what he called "the Augustine–Bonaventure tradition" and against the "Aristotle–Thomas Aquinas tradition" in theology. There have been many others throughout history who have found Bonaventure to be a winning figure. "He never condemns the opinions of others and emphatically disclaims anything like finality for his own views." Thus wrote the Catholic historian Paschal Robinson, also a Franciscan, about Bonaventure eighty years ago. They are words, however, that might equally be applied to Boff, who never claims to offer something new, and who always seems to be trying to find some value even in theologies quite different from his own. "Indeed," Robinson continues in his discussion of Bonaventure, "he asserts the littleness of his authority, renounces all claims to originality and calls himself a 'poor compiler.'" Boff, too, thinks of himself as drawing together the teachings of the bishops and popes and applying them to the Latin American situation. He does not strain to be creative or original the way, for example, Hans Küng sometimes does.

Boff and Bonaventure both have an engaging, unpretentious way of writing. This style led some of Bonaventure's later disciples to contrast him favorably with the ponderousness of certain scholastic thinkers. One such admirer, the great French theologian and preacher Jean Charlier de Gerson (1363–1429), wrote, for example, "one does not find in his pages vain trifles or useless cavils ... or worldly digressions. ... This is the reason why St. Bonaventure has been abandoned by those Scholastics who are devoid of piety of whom the number is alas! but too large." A similar simplicity of expression has led some of Boff's detractors to call him a journalist or a mere popularizer.

Recent historians of theology have questioned the tendency to set Bonaventure against the scholastics. But there are some important differences between the two schools that could cast some light on the dispute between Boff and Ratzinger. Bonaventure, as a faithful follower of St. Francis, strongly believed in the presence of the Spirit of God within all creatures. He therefore insisted on the possibility of experiencing God directly. He did not accept the familiar scholastic theological idea, elaborated by his contemporary St. Thomas Aquinas, that we cannot know God directly but must begin with the created works, God's "effects," and then make our way step by upward step to their divine Author. Indeed, for Bonaventure, all human acts in the everyday world, whatever they are directed toward, are expressions of "an uncreated divine light." This is true even when we are unaware that it is the uncreated light of God within us that enables us to act, to know, and to make judgments about what is good or right or true.

We can glimpse the inner struggle of Bonaventure in his theol-

ogy. The follower of a saint who ranked living among the poor far
higher than studying learned texts, he tried to translate a spiritual
intuition into discursive idiom. His theology is both mystical and
intellectual. We can also see trouble ahead. St. Thomas taught
that the mind's ascent up the long ladder of "effects" could never
quite reach to God. Something else would eventually be needed to
close the gap. For Thomas, the bridge was provided by the church,
the sole custodian of revealed truth, the only trustworthy bridge
between knowledge and faith. For Bonaventure, on the other hand,
the church means something else. Rather than the ladder between
the pinnacle of earth and the lowest gate of heaven, he sees the
church more as a party of pilgrims, seeking to follow Christ, sus-
tained by the sacraments and constantly becoming more aware of
the source of the inner light that makes them human. It is not
hard to discern what hovers behind these two visions: for Thomas
it is the tiered universe of Aristotle's metaphysics, for Bonaventure,
Francis's jaunty band of beggars. This difference in their images
of the church that divides Bonaventure and Thomas Aquinas and
their respective followers from each other has never been definitively settled. The trouble ahead was that in a church that welcomed a variety of theologies, the two images could co-exist. But
as the church began to insist on doctrinal univocality the two were
bound to clash.

What is the church? For those who follow Aquinas, an authoritative hierarchy that is the repository of revelation seems logically
essential to span the gulf between knowledge and faith. For those
who think more like Bonaventure, the result is quite different. A
hierarchy may be useful, even vital. But if our knowledge of the
world is made possible by a God who is already present within
the world and within every person, then the community of faith
and ultimately the whole family of creation become the medium
of the divine. I think this hoary old dispute, argued so eloquently
in the thirteenth century by these two titans of theology, helps
explain the present controversy between Boff and the liberation
theologians on the one hand and their Vatican critics on the other.
Innocent III and St. Francis have never really come to terms.

There are other long-standing theological debates that cast
their shadows over the present one. As Franciscans, for example, both Boff and Bonaventure are fascinated by the Christ of
the gospel stories as a moral exemplar. For Bonaventure, Christ

touches the moral life in three ways. First, he removes disabling guilt, which modern psychologists would probably agree is a major prerequisite to any mature moral life. Second, he provides an inviting example of how life should be lived, what today might be called a "role model." Third, by grace, Christ helps people to "follow" him, to live in some measure as he lived. Boff continues to see Jesus in this light, and his most widely read book, *Jesus Christ, Liberator,* is thoroughly "Franciscan" in its treatment of the historical life of Christ.

In contrast to the importance of the theme of discipleship — following Jesus — among Franciscans, one finds hardly any discussion of it at all in the voluminous theology of Thomas Aquinas. This is also true of Cardinal Ratzinger. In his thoughtful writing on Jesus, the prefect prefers to concentrate not on the prophet of Nazareth, but on the passion and sacrificial death of the divine Son of God. The difference is a matter of emphasis rather than substance, but we will notice it time and again in disputes between Rome and the Latin Americans about just how much the earthly life of Jesus should shape the church's work today.

It is also important to notice that Bonaventure was talking about the actual removal of guilt from the Christian's life. He was not propounding the so-called juridical view of forgiveness made prominent later by some Protestant theologies in which, despite the fact that God forgives, sin remains almost as serious an obstacle to morality as ever. As Luther put it, explaining that point of view, we are always *simul iustus et peccator.* For Bonaventure, however, a certain measure of moral and spiritual progress is possible since Christ gradually purges and obliterates — over the course of life — that which separates human beings from God and their fellow creatures.

This Franciscan view of the significance of Jesus for life in a sinful and imperfect world surfaces again in the current controversy when the liberationists are accused of "utopianism." Bonaventure believed Christ actually removes sin and guilt rather than simply forgiving them. This makes him a theological progenitor of the idea of "sanctification," a central theme in the later theology of John Wesley and Methodism. But it also links him to those who believe people can hope and work for real change in society as well as in individuals. (The Argentine Methodist theologian José Míguez-Bonino believes the doctrine of sanctification, shorn of its later individualistic distortions, could provide a useful bridge between Protestants, including Pentecostalists, and Catholic liberation theology.[2])

Like the liberation theologians today, Bonaventure grounded the idea of sanctification in apostolic poverty. Indeed in 1269, just a few years before his death, Bonaventure had to answer yet another charge against the Franciscans, this one written by one Master Gerard of Abbeville, entitled *Against the Adversary of Christian Perfection.* Abbeville ridiculed the Franciscans' belief that Christ's call for evangelical poverty should be taken literally, and he questioned the idea that God's grace allows anyone to progress toward the perfection of Christ in this life. It is worth remembering this dispute, and Bonaventure's response, which he called *The Apology of the Poor,* when we remember that liberation theologians, like the early Franciscans, are often taken to task for their allegedly romantic view of the poor and their purported utopianism.[3] But Bonaventure, who was neither a romantic nor a utopian, held the same views 600 years ago.

6.

Charism and Power

Boff's own theology includes more than just equal parts of Francis and Bonaventure, of course. It begins with the Bible and the church fathers, and is flavored with more than a dash of modern French and German theology and social analysis. This is all poured then into the seething broth of contemporary Latin America, particularly Brazil. He links the radical gospel spirit of Assisi with the driving energy and prodigious poverty of the *favelas* of Rio, São Paulo, and Bahia. But he joins them with both mind and heart. He is a friar with the mind of a theologian. And he is a theologian with the heart of a friar. This is a formidable combination of qualities, and Boff called on them all in the contest of scholarly wits to which he was summoned in Rome.

The Franciscans have never been easy marks in a fight. Their spare simplicity produces a certain agility and toughness. The men who hiked all over Europe in tonsures and sandals calling on the rich to give their treasures away, and denouncing the unseemly opulence of the papacy, were not softies. Boff has inherited some of this hardy willingness to pick up a gauntlet when it is flung down. One suspects that although he did not initiate the quarrel with Ratzinger, he was perfectly willing to take it on when it got started. There is also some evidence that the cardinal expected him neither to mobilize his allies so quickly, nor to fight back quite so vigorously when he received the first letter from Rome. But he did, and this is what makes reading through the sixty-seven-page document he took with him to present to the Congregation for the Doctrine of the Faith so valuable. It is a highly distilled portrait of Boff under pressure, an example of how the friar-theologian's mind works when he is on the spot.

In one sense, Boff knew the prefect had called upon him to

defend the indefensible. The book he was challenged to vindicate, *Church: Charism and Power,* is an uneven paste-up of speeches, articles written originally in French, German, Spanish, and Portuguese, and assorted lecture notes dating back to 1974. It even includes a chunk lifted bodily out of the doctoral dissertation that he wrote in the early 1970s, which was published in German by Paderborn in 1972, under the imposing title *Die Kirche als Sakrament im Horizon der Welterfahrung* (The Church as Sacrament in the Horizon of World Experience). The excerpt from the dissertation constitutes only one of the book's thirteen chapters, but any scholar can imagine the queasiness Boff must have felt when called upon, twelve years after its publication, suddenly once again to defend a dissertation only part of which contributes to the present argument. Consider also that the ultimate authority university faculties command over their students is the power to flunk them. The Congregation for the Doctrine of the Faith has at its disposal other and considerably more formidable means of expressing its misgivings.

Still, the field of honor having been staked out for him, Boff's preparatory notes indicate he entered it with relish. Some of the thrusts and parries he carries off in his prepared reply must even have secretly pleased Ratzinger, himself no stranger to the jousting of seminar rooms. For example, the cardinal knows how much Boff emphasizes starting theology "from the bottom up," that is, from the experience of the poor Christians of the base communities; so in his letter, he slyly twits the Brazilian for relying too heavily on certain current European theologians "who are also, sadly, being examined at the moment." The scholars the prefect is referring to are Gotthold Hasenhüttl, a Catholic dogmatic theologian at the University of Saarbrucken, whose book on ordination, published in 1969, Boff cites eight times, and Rome's longtime favorite problem child, Hans Küng.

Boff's return cut is a beauty. He deftly points out that in the introduction to the work cited, Professor Hasenhüttl includes a generous note of thanks for all the helpful suggestions he received from (then) Professor Joseph Ratzinger, and that the book itself appears in a series called *Okumenische Forschungen* (Ecumenical Research) guided and edited by Joseph Ratzinger and none other than Hans Küng. As for quoting Küng, whom Boff cites seven times, he reminds Ratzinger that in the prefect's own book on the church, *Das Neue Volk Gottes* (Dusseldorf, 1969), he cites Küng a total of eleven times.

Ratzinger had complained not only that Boff relies on these usual suspects but also that he ignores the body of teachings of the church's Magisterium itself. In answer to this accusation Boff demonstrates that, when called upon, he can be just as pedantic as anyone else. There are in his book, he drily recounts, "228 citations from scriptural scholars; 120 from the Gospel; 45 from the Old and New Testaments.... Besides there are 13 references to St. Augustine; and others to Ignatius of Antioch; Leo the Great; Clement of Rome; etc."

Boff's "etc." might have put the whole question into proper perspective. But having got into the swing of it, he also adds that he quoted recent popes 52 times; the Vatican Council 79 times; the Latin American bishops' Puebla document 78 times; plus assorted encyclicals such as *Octogesima Adveniens, Redemptor Hominis,* and others.

At first this sounds like the scholarly equivalent of a Sumo wrestler bowing to his opponent and then in the direction of the imperial palace before the match. In Boff's case, however, it is hard to believe he piled up all this footnote arithmetic in anything but a somewhat playful spirit. The cascade of figures lends a needed bit of comic relief to what was after all a serious occasion.

Besides their feistiness, another feature of Franciscans is loyalty to the papal *office* combined with limitless fury toward the evil persons who sometimes occupy it. The ambivalence runs deeper than it does in some other orders. The Jesuits, for example, make a special extra pledge of obedience to the pontiff, but from their earliest days the worldly-wise descendants of Ignatius Loyola have accepted a certain degree of ecclesial corruption with stoic resignation: the world being what it is, there will always be the occasional mendacious pope. The Franciscans on the other hand were founded by a man who wanted everyone to walk in the footsteps of the poor Christ, and during its first decades some members of the movement even came to believe that they should replace the wicked and worldly papal court as the authentic representatives of the gospel. Boff, of course, has no such hopes. But in the paper he took along to Rome, parts of which he read to Ratzinger, Boff could not resist tapping into this muckraking tradition. He did so because outrageous stories about the sadists and hedonists who have sometimes sullied the seat of Peter, though tedious to nearly everyone by now, lend a special punch to the distinction Boff repeatedly makes between the legitimacy of ecclesial offices themselves and the wrongness of their frequent misuse.

The point is an important one, but some readers of Boff's notes might legitimately decide that he overdid it. For example, was it really necessary for him to mention the grisly story of Pope Formosus (891–896), whose body was literally dug up by the notorious Pope Stephen VI? Boff reminds the prefect and the staff of the Congregation for the Doctrine of the Faith, using the eminent Catholic historian Henri Daniel-Rops as his source, that the corpse of the old pope was taken from the tomb and seated on a chair to be judged by a synod presided over by the new pope. Accusers then pointed to the decaying cadaver and recalled Pope Formosus's intrigues and his violations of canon law. A terrified lower cleric was instructed to speak for the dead man and confess his faults. Then, as this ecclesial Grand Guignol unfolded, the judges ripped off the deceased pope's pontifical vestments and "took with them pieces of his putrefied body." Then "they cut off the fingers of his right hand — those fingers that had blessed the faithful and . . . the body was given to the people and thrown into the river." Boff spares no details and in his notes he puts this edifying little tale between a mention of Benedict IX (1033–1045), who was elevated to the papacy at the age of twelve, and a passing reference to the Renaissance popes whose careers he says, in a momentary lapse into understatement, "do not speak well of the exercise of power according to the dictums of the gospel." He resists the temptation to add another "etc."

Why does a normally fresh and forward-looking writer like Boff fall so enthusiastically into the tired old sport of bad-pope bashing? Stories of the cruel, greedy, and promiscuous pontiffs of the nasty days of yore are hardly shocking anymore. Why dredge them up? Perhaps here, also, Boff's edgy Franciscan spirituality may help explain what to some might sound merely gratuitous. Many Catholics believe that, in an odd way, the endurance of the papal office despite the villains, rakes, and debauchers who have occupied it provides a kind of inverse proof of God's providence. No merely human institution, it is argued, could have survived so many rascals. For the Franciscans, however, the stories of the bad popes have another moral: that power corrupts, and that this includes religious power. Franciscan spirituality opposes worldly wealth and privilege, especially when it seeps into the church, not just because it is unjust but because Franciscans believe it rots the fiber of those who hold it. It deprives them of the joy of salvation. Francis was no dour Savonarola. He urged people to cast off their fine raiment and give away their gold, not for grimly ascetical reasons, but in order to be blessed, happy, and free. For the Franciscans, the bad popes teach us that even those one might expect to be most carefully safeguarded by Divine Providence are also subject to irresistible temptation when given too much power. To rephrase Acton's dictum *à la* St. Francis, "power corrupts but infallible power corrupts infallibly."

Boff reiterates in his reply to the prefect that he does not drag out these seamy stories to embarrass anyone. He does it to make his point: that what needs to be converted in the church is not just the individuals who wield power but the *pattern* of power distribution in the institutional church. He uses the gothic tales to drive home his key thesis — that there must be room for the spirit in the church and that the comparatively recent centralization of more and more power in Rome makes it hard for the Spirit to carry out a renewing function. The bad popes are not bad people but the victims of a bad system.

Boff makes the same argument in the book itself. As the title suggests, *Church: Charism and Power* does have a theme — the tension of charism and power, spirit and structure, in the church. The charism it speaks of has little to do with the so-called charismatic movement of healing and "speaking in tongues" that gained some prominence in the Catholic church in the 1970s and early 1980s. Nor does it refer (as the word is used today) to a certain kind of photogenic glamor. "Charism" simply means gift. Boff uses it to refer to the different "gifts" the Spirit of God gives the people who constitute the church. Some scholars believe "charismata" (plural) originally described the booty a military commander handed out to his troops after defeating a rival city and sacking it of its goods. The "charismata" were the fruits of conquest: slaves, precious articles, jewelry, and no doubt women wrenched from the losers.

St. Paul describes these gifts in the First Epistle to the Corinthians. For the Apostle, who had a knack for using ordinary language, including military terms, with a different twist, the "charisms"

came to mean the capacities God gives people to enable them to
serve. It means "gift" in a sense closer to the way we describe
a talented person as a "gifted" musician or writer. But for St.
Paul, and also for Boff, a charism, or gift, has the exclusive purpose of helping its recipient to do God's work in the world. A
charism is a talent someone recognizes as a gift, and not as some
sort of personal achievement. In St. Paul's view, God has with-
held none of the spiritual spoils, but has distributed many different
charisms — teaching, serving, helping the poor, preaching, admin-
istering. Indeed no one is left out of the largesse. As St. Paul puts
it, "each one has his own gift [charism] from God, one this and another that" (1 Cor. 7:7). As Boff reads this, it means, "There are
no passive members in the Church. Each person, within the body,
exercises some function. Therefore, every Christian," he concludes,
"is charismatic."[1]

But Boff is anything but an ecclesial anarchist. He knows that
a congregation, a church, or indeed a whole society made up of
"gifted" individuals each trying to express some charism would
create an unbearable cacophony. Some charisms would inevitably
drown out others. St. Paul says the charisms must be used "for
the common good" (1 Cor. 12:7), and Boff asks, "What would the
church be if there were a multiplicity of charisms without any order
among them? How would all the members constitute one body, if
there were no one to see that the charisms were exercised for the
common good?"[2] This is where *power*, the second key word in the
title, comes in. For Boff the church must contain *both* charisms and
power. If he is not an anarchist, neither is he a Quaker or a free-
floating mystic. As a Franciscan, Boff knows that the saint from
Assisi, one of the most "charismatic" figures in all religious history,
nevertheless prepared a *Rule* for his new movement and demanded
the brothers follow it. St. Francis was not averse to using power.
After his death, stories circulated of how severe he could be with
friars who got out of line. Once, according to legend, he forced an
unlucky one who had lied to chew up a handful of manure. Boff
believes since there must be order within the church, ecclesiastical
power is not bad or even merely neutral. "Power," he says, "can
be a charism." But he quickly adds, "as long as it serves everyone
and is an instrument for building justice in the community."[3]

There is no necessary contradiction between charism and power,
either in the church or in the society at large. In fact the gift for

promoting unity and harmony among all the diverse charisms is an indispensable charism in the church. This is the gift the church recognizes in those it makes its leaders. In the Catholic church these leaders constitute what is called the hierarchy. But as Boff correctly points out, the New Testament, in saying what these leaders should be called, allows scarcely any hint of domination or privilege. Those designated to maintain harmony and order in the early church were not even given religious titles, even though they were available in the language at the time. The word for bishop (*episkopos*) merely meant "overseer" and deacon (*diakonos*) meant "servant." Both were secular terms. Significantly — although Boff does not mention this himself — the word "priest," which did have religious overtones in the first two centuries, is used in the New Testament to refer only to the Jewish priesthood, to Christ himself, and to the whole "people of God" (everyone in the church). It is not applied to individual Christian leaders. That came later. Still, there is the gift of power, and it is the rightful responsibility of those who hold it to exercise it.

This all sounds so sensible one has to ask again why *Church: Charism and Power* kicked up such a brouhaha. In short, Boff irked many in the hierarchy by charging that although the exercise of power within the church *need* not violate its essential nature, it often does. Very often. The way he documents this misuse of power goes a long way in explaining the angry responses to the book. To the people who hold sacral power in the church, the vigor with which Boff sets out to show *why* and *how much* it is misused must have seemed relentless, if not ruthless. But this is the irony. Boff's stated purpose is precisely to remove the onus from the leaders themselves. He does this by carefully distinguishing between the *individual persons* who wield sacred authority, most of whom he agrees are honest and fair-minded, and the *organizational pattern* within which they must work, which he deems flawed and sclerotic. The latter he calls the "church institution."

Boff knows there was probably never a day when someone was not abusing churchly power. But he believes the pattern itself was fundamentally altered for the worse at the time of Emperor Constantine's conversion and the subsequent transformation of Christianity from an illegal cult (*religio illicita*) into both the official religion of the Roman empire and its sacred ideology. But even here, unlike some more radical Christian historians, Boff does not view this immense change in the legal status of Christianity as something entirely negative. As a theologian who believes the strength of Catholicism lies in its willingness to enter into and embrace human cultures, he does not see the conversion of Constantine as a tragic "second fall" (as some of the Protestant reformers did). He views it, rather, as an event that presented the church with the opportunity to cease being a ghetto sect and become a true *ecclesia universalis*. The emperor's conversion was the invitation to an adventure, a chance to transform power by using it in the light of the gospel images of servanthood, compassion, and equality. It opened the door for the creation of a new humanism, even of a new politics.

But, for Boff, the church missed its big chance. Instead of transforming the existing order, it merely adapted itself to it. It provided the empire with a sacred ideology, and just in the nick of time since belief in Juno, Zeus, and the other gods of the Roman pantheon was in decline. Sadly, however, when the leaders of the empire joined the church, Boff asserts, "a paganization of Christianity took place, and not a Christianization of paganism." It could have gone the other way, but instead the church took on the empire's institutions: its law, its bureaucratic centralization, its ranks and titles. Even the terms used to describe the church's organization — "diocese" and "parish" — were absorbed directly from the empire. Boff says this set the church "on a path of power that continues today and that we must hasten to end."[4]

What is this "path of power" that must be ended? Again it should be emphasized that Boff believes power is a "charism" and is absolutely essential in the church. The damage comes, he says, because of the confusion between the *kind* of power Jesus himself used and urged upon his disciples, which Boff describes with the New Testament Greek word *exousia,* and the kind of power that characterized imperial Roman officialdom, which he symbolizes with the Latin word *potestas.* The difference is enormous. The power Jesus used is the power to love. He explicitly warned his disciples *not* to "lord it over others as the heathen [the Romans] do," but "to become like servants" (Mark 10:42–44). When Jesus said he was "given all power in heaven and on earth" (Matt. 28:18) and then passed this power on to the apostles, Boff says, it was not *potestas*, the power to dominate and rule, but "an astound-

ing power to be patient and support even ingrates and evil-doers."
The power of love, says Boff,

> is different in nature from the power of domination; it is frag-
> ile, vulnerable, conquering through its weakness and its ca-
> pacity for giving and forgiveness. Jesus always demonstrated
> this *exousia* in his life.[5]

The church had a chance to demonstrate this kind of power when
it became legal and established. But it did not. Instead, *potestas*
became the prevailing form of power within the church as well as
in the empire.

For Boff, *potestas* is the cancer in the body of Christ. Its inner logic, especially when it is sacralized by religious symbols, is
malignant. Instead of encouraging unity it inevitably divides the
rulers from the ruled. In the Catholic church this division became a breach between the clergy, in whose hands more and more
"power" was vested, and the ordinary laity, who became passive
objects of the *potestas* the clergy exercised. The tragic result was
that slowly but inexorably the charismatic essence of the church,
in which everyone has a gift to offer, was squeezed out. "Christianity," says Boff, "is not against power in itself but its diabolical
forms which show themselves as dominion and control." It is this
"diabolical form" of power that, having stolen into the church, now
threatens to destroy it.

In the most controversial parts of *Church: Charism and Power*,
Boff describes the damaging way power is actually used, or misused, in the visible organization called "the Catholic church." On
these pages Boff is not describing the mystical body as it *ought* to
be, but the actual *modus operandi* of the institutional church. So
he feels perfectly free to draw on the tools of organizational analysis. This is what raised so many eyebrows, especially when he
writes, for example, that in the unequal and asymmetric relationship that has emerged in the church, the ruling stratum "produces
the symbolic goods and the other consumes them." However it
may be rationalized by theological theory, he says, the observable
fact is that the ordained class (the clergy) makes all the decisions
and develops theologies that justify its monopoly by attributing its
power to a divine origin. What actually happens is the domination
of some by others, just what Jesus warned against. "The authority

of the church," Boff insists, "exists and is willed by God." About
that there is no argument. What is at issue is the institutional
form this authority has taken, which Boff considers a plain denial
of Christ's teachings.[6]

Boff believes this anomaly in the church's interior life gives
rise to a series of contradictions that cripple its mission. He cata-
logs them unsparingly. For example, although the church criticizes
censorship and the lack of press freedom in society, the hierarchy
"exerts almost inquisitorial control of the Catholic means of communication." The Vatican forcefully speaks out for human rights
in the secular world; but the Congregation for the Doctrine of the
Faith continues to rely on procedures that are unacceptable in civil
society. Thus, in dealing with a theologian suspected of heresy, it
can begin its work without notifying the accused, who does not
have access to all the proceedings, and, in any case, has no right
to independent counsel. (A *relator pro auctore* is sometimes appointed for him, but the accused has no say in who it is.) Boff
calls this "a Kafkaesque process wherein the accuser, the defender,
the lawyer, and the judge are one and the same."[7] Many church
documents defend the rights of women. But the hierarchy will not
allow them to become priests or, in some places, even to speak in
church or help serve communion. All this, of course, conspires to
render the church highly suspect when it proclaims its support for
human rights in society.

The point, for Boff, is that the solution must go far beyond
merely exhorting the individuals who work within the Catholic
religious system to be fairer or more high-minded. A conversion
is indeed needed. But it must be a conversion of the institutional
system itself. Boff's hope is not to bring the church "up to date"
or to put it more in line with modern models. Rather, it is to align
it more closely with the gospel. Boff is an evangelical radical, not
a modernist. To confuse the two is to miss his point completely.

In this no-nonsense discussion of the institutional church and its
misuse of power *ad intra* Boff paints such an unattractive picture
that one can well see why many people in the hierarchy, including
some Brazilians, thought he should be brought quickly to heel.
Also, in summing it all up, in a chapter called "The Power of the
Institutional Church: Can It Be Converted?" (which is drawn from
an address he gave to a conference of Christian base communities
in Pôrto Alegre in 1974), he wrote an all-too-quotable sentence

that not only caused immense consternation, but probably pushed his critics over the edge. "It is strange to see," he writes, "that the Church institution has developed into exactly that which Christ did not want it to be."[8]

These are certainly fighting words. As far as some bishops and prefects are concerned they represent rank and unvarnished heresy. But as the dispute became public such sentences (and there are a few other dandies like it) were frequently quoted in isolation and without reference to the careful argument Boff had crafted about forms of power. Also, the offending phrases were often published without indicating that they appeared in an article in which Boff forcibly argued that, despite everything — the church *can* change, that it does have the capacity to reform itself, that it can reappropriate a more gospel-based style of governance and a kind of power that — though never perfect — can come closer to *exousia* than to *potestas*.

As we shall notice in a moment when we turn to Cardinal Ratzinger, both he and Boff are convinced that all is not well in the church. But they hold quite disparate ideas about what is wrong and what must be done to heal the pathology. Ratzinger believes the situation is one of rapid centrifugal disintegration: the center will not hold, and what is needed is "recentrage." For Boff there is a decadence of a different sort: power has become *too* centralized. Therefore, what is needed is "to recreate a model for the institutional Church because the model of power has given all it has to give."[9] Ratzinger assays the crisis as a classically trained theologian whose progressive bent did not survive the ugly student tumult in the German universities during the 1960s. He views the Catholic world as the bishop of an exemplary conservative Catholic region who became prefect of the Congregation for the Doctrine of the Faith just as many of his closest associates began to fear that the changes initiated by Vatican II had curdled into excess.

Conversely, Boff sees the same period of history from the perspective of a disenfranchised people on the periphery of Christendom, who in the past twenty years have lived through a wholly unexpected renaissance of Catholic faith, not at all through a disaster. Boff works in a part of the church where Vatican II did not mark the start of a deadly decline, but rather the beginning of a new life. Europe, except for Poland, has watched a steady falling off in the number of young men entering the priesthood, but Brazil has had an increase. Finally, Boff reads this history as a Franciscan whose tradition has always harbored a suspicion of the worldly power, wealth, and influence of Rome and has constantly reintroduced an alternative vision of a church rooted in love rather than in *potestas*.

The influence of St. Francis and St. Bonaventure shines through with particular clarity when Boff spells out what he means by the reform the church needs. "The attitude of the institution," he writes, "must be one of conversion, with everything that term implies: poverty, rejection of false security, acceptance of the inability to control the future...."[10] The conversion Boff envisages would be more like Francis's than like Constantine's. It would require the whole church, but especially those with the charism of unity and administration, to begin looking at the sources of faith (Jesus and the Gospels), not through the eyes of earthly rulers, but with the eyes of those who have been denied that perspective, that is, the poor. When this happens, Boff is sure that the "cause of Christ, of the historical Jesus who was poor, weak, powerless, critical of the social and religious status quo of his time,"[11] will shine forth again. This passage sums up Boff's understanding of his own vocation as theologian: he is trying to help the church "seek a new presence in the world and avoid...the pitfalls of yesteryear." His is the classical Franciscan vision of a spiritually renewed church applied to the contemporary world.

The issue is whether such a "conversion of the church" is possible. Boff insists it is because he believes he actually sees it happening around him. He does not have to accept it by blind faith. Through sharing the life of the powerless Christians in the slums and shantytowns of Latin America, many priests, nuns, bishops, and even theologians have already learned to hear the gospel with new ears. But for Cardinal Ratzinger and his curial colleagues, however much they might pray for and dream of a real conversion of the church, they have long since had to concede that, from where they sit, it seems quite improbable. Consequently, however much they might like to opt for the loving *exousia* Jesus exemplified, they feel that, given the imperfect church and fallen world in which we live, they must reluctantly settle for a power somewhat closer to *potestas*. The situation has an element of pathos. The prefect and his supporters, in their own eyes as well as in Boff's, are thoughtful men and serious Christians who are earnestly trying to do their best. What must upset them most about Boff's buoyant vision is that they would love to be able to share it. But they cannot. Therefore they regretfully concede that it must be discouraged, lest that necessary but less-than-ideal edifice of church *potestas* be undermined and everyone be left with nothing.

7

Brazilians in Rome

Boff wanted his time in the Franciscan General Curia to be one of undisturbed preparation and thought. But it was not. On September 3, just one day after he arrived in Rome, the same Sacred Congregation for the Doctrine of the Faith that had summoned him, suddenly and without previous warning, published its long-awaited "Instruction on Certain Aspects of the 'Theology of Liberation.'" It was not good news for Boff and his co-workers.

It is not entirely clear why such an important document, which criticized several facets of the movement Boff is associated with, was released on this particular day. Vatican officials insisted that, as improbable as it seems, the timing was accidental; that the Instruction had been in preparation for some months and that it was simply ready for publication. They resolutely denied that Boff's presence in Rome had anything to do with it. Others, who are aware of the Vatican's frequent use of one occasion or another — a saint's day, a visit, a commemoration — to underline a certain message, have their doubts. In any case, the press naturally associated Boff's arrival in Rome for the "colloquy" with the sharp criticisms the Instruction made of liberation theology. Once again, Boff was besieged by phone calls and requests for interviews about his view of the new document. He turned them all down and asked his brother to explain why he did not feel it appropriate to respond at that point.

Of course, Boff did take the time to sit at his small desk in the General Curia and read the thirty-six-page Instruction, especially since he knew Cardinal Ratzinger had written most of it. A few months later, he wrote that as he read it, he felt a variety of emotions one after another. At first he was pleased not only that the Congregation for the Doctrine of the Faith had taken the liberation theology movement so seriously but had even, for the first time, acknowledged the validity of the enterprise. "In itself," the Instruction says in an early section, "the expression 'theology of liberation' is a thoroughly valid term: It designates a theological reflection centered on the biblical theme of liberation and freedom, and on the urgency of its practical realization."[1] But as he read on, Boff reports that he became progressively uneasy and disappointed. The Instruction, even in its recognition of the need for such a theology, somehow made what he and his colleagues were doing sound elevated and cerebral, removed from the people for whom it was intended. Boff later characterized the Instruction's point of view as "extrinsic." He said the document conveyed a sense of musty tranquility and gave no evidence that its writer had any feel whatever for the conflict-ridden continent from which the liberation theology movement had arisen.

When he got to the meat of the Instruction Boff must have shifted uneasily. It appeared to him, he later wrote, that its author had forgotten the important strides Vatican II had taken in such areas as biblical study and the meaning of historical change for theology. When he came to the long section criticizing liberation theology for its "uncritical use of Marxist modes of analysis," Boff says he began to wonder just who the writer had in mind. The description fit no liberation theologian he knew. It seemed to be an attack on a carelessly assembled straw man. The "Marxism" it described sounded more like the stale orthodoxy that in most of Latin America is defended only by small academic cliques who — in any case — have only contempt for liberation theology. Boff also says that what bothered him most about it was not what it said but what it did not. What he found missing was thirty years of turbulent Latin American history, years in which priests and laypeople and at least one bishop had died for the faith, and a church had been reborn. He had lived through that history, and the writers of this tract had not. Sobered by his perusal of the Instruction, he put it in a desk drawer and continued to prepare himself for the colloquy.

On the following day, September 3, two visitors called on Boff in his quarters. One was Father Joseph Clemens, the private secretary of Cardinal Ratzinger. He was accompanied by Father Eugenio X. Aramburu, a theologian associated with the Sacred Congregation. The two men told Boff they were deeply concerned about the press reports of his visit. They complained that the newspapers were wrongly alleging that the Sacred Congregation had revived the same methods that had been applied in recent years to theologians Edward Schillebeeckx and Hans Küng. They assured Boff that his case was something entirely different, that it would involve nothing more than a "clarifying conversation" with Cardinal Ratzinger. They then offered to pick him up in a car that Friday for the conversation. Boff thanked them, but said he preferred to be driven there by his Franciscan brothers and accompanied by the Franciscan minister general who had already volunteered to do so. The representatives of the Sacred Congregation, however, told him they did not believe that arrangement would be appropriate, so the matter of how Boff would be delivered to the colloquy was left to be settled by the Franciscan minister general and Cardinal Ratzinger. Somewhat later, after he had consulted with the prefect, Boff's superior told him that he would be driven to the headquarters of the Sacred Congregation by Cardinal Ratzinger's own secretary. None of his fellow Franciscans would be permitted to ride along.

During the days while these preparations were being made, the two Brazilian bishops with whom Boff had conferred before leaving his homeland, Cardinal Aloísio Lorscheider and Bishop Ivo Lorscheiter (who is president of the Brazilian Bishops' Conference), also landed in Rome. All public announcements of their arrival stated that they were present on regular church business and carefully avoided any mention of Boff. The two bishops attended to other duties, but when they were received by the pope, they raised the issue of Boff. Boff's friends told him later that, in the course of their conversation, John Paul II informed them he had read a number of Boff's books *"com agrado"* but had not yet read the book under investigation. The phrase *"com agrado"* in Portuguese, the language in which Boff reported the bishops' conversation and presumably the language in which the multi-lingual pope was speaking, is an ambiguous one. It can mean either "with pleasure" or "with agreement." Whichever nuance was intended it was clear to the bishops that the pope himself had no questions he wanted to raise, at least about any of Boff's previous books.

After their visit with the pope, the two bishops also paid a call on Cardinal Ratzinger and asked his permission to be present at the colloquy with Boff. The cardinal, however, told them that since there was no provision for such attendance in the *Ratio Agendi,* the relevant code of canon law for such procedures, and since it might create an undesirable precedent, he could not comply with their request. Cardinal Lorscheider did not agree. He claimed that as president of the Commission on Doctrine of Brazil he had the right to be present *ex officio.* Ratzinger then told him that since they differed on this matter, the question would have to be referred to the Vatican secretary of state, Cardinal Agostino Casaroli. When they asked about the actual procedure for the colloquy, Ratzinger told the bishops it would take place in one of the rooms of the headquarters of the Sacred Congregation and that there would be a notary there in the person of an Argentine priest named Jorge Mejía. Boff would be permitted to examine the record, suggest modifications, and then sign it.

Before the Brazilians left, Ratzinger gave them one more piece of information, which, when they reported it to Boff later that day, came as a rude surprise. The colloquy was not to be a "conversation" as Boff thought the emissaries of the cardinal had just promised. Rather, it would be more in the nature of the interrogation to which Edward Schillebeeckx had been subjected four years before. When he heard this, Boff immediately went to the library and looked up the record of the Schillebeeckx case and studied it for most of one day.

Meanwhile yet another Brazilian bishop had arrived in Rome: Boff's friend, former teacher, and lifelong mentor Cardinal Paulo Evaristo Arns, the archbishop of São Paulo. He told reporters he was in the city "on routine business." But he also made known his desire to be present at the colloquy. Boff later wrote that Arns told him he wanted to be present so that he could "testify to the ecclesial character of this theology, which had been fashioned in Brazil, in strict conformity with the bishops of that country and with their long-range pastoral commitment." These are Boff's words, and he may be putting Arns's sentiments in the most favorable language. But it is certain that however he may have expressed it himself, Arns — who is probably the most widely respected bishop in Latin America — was on Boff's side. Whatever other errands might have brought him to Rome, he was also clearly there to support Boff.

Now there were three highly-placed Brazilian bishops in the Holy City, two of them members of the College of Cardinals, all there ostensibly for purposes independent of the Boff colloquy but all seeking ways to be present at it. At this point, since the prefect continued to oppose any such participation, his suggestion of an appeal to the Vatican secretary of state, Agostino Casaroli, seemed to offer the only solution to the impasse, so the bishops went to see him. Casaroli received his fellow bishops and cardinals amiably and expressed his understanding of their reasons for wanting to be present at the colloquy. He then offered what to him seemed to be a reasonable compromise. There would be, he suggested, two meetings instead of one. At the first only Boff and Ratzinger (and the notary) would be present. It would not be a regular "colloquy" in the usual sense of the Sacred Congregation but a conversation between the two men strictly for the purpose of clarifying certain issues. Later the same day there would be a second conversation in which the Brazilian bishops would also be invited to participate. Everyone accepted the new arrangement as a way out.

But the trouble was not yet over. While the Brazilian bishops were negotiating the form of the colloquy with the Vatican secretary of state, the newspapers in Rome published a story, which also appeared later in the semi-official Vatican newspaper *L'Osservatore Romano*. The article quoted Cardinal Ratzinger as saying that Boff's presence in Rome was at Boff's own initiative and that he was present merely to "confer" with the Sacred Congregation about the debate he had touched off in Brazil. Boff asked Cardinal Lorscheider if he could find out from Ratzinger's office how this report had been initiated. The office told Lorscheider they would have it corrected immediately, but also told him to convey to Father Boff the information that his colloquy was now scheduled not for September 8, as the papal nuncio in Brazil had said, but for September 7. What no one in the Sacred Congregation, for all its sensitivity to symbolism, had apparently noticed, is that September 7 is Brazilian independence day.

8

The Brazilian Church and Roman Intervention

Leonardo Boff knows full well that the independence of his homeland, which came in 1822 and which he celebrated in Rome on the day of his colloquy, did not make the Brazilian church free of Portuguese or European domination. It continued to be an appendage, albeit a somewhat neglected one. Only after effective papal authority was established in the late nineteenth century did Brazilians find themselves drawn onto the far edge of a centralized ecclesial structure, which energetically promoted a pastoral strategy devised not by Latin Americans but by Europeans, most of whom had never set foot on their continent. To many Brazilians, that strategy seems to have been a colossal failure. This is why they are so resentful of Rome's continuing attempt to dominate and second-guess them.

Rome's strategy in establishing authority was in effect a quid-pro-quo arrangement with the rulers of civil society, though, from its point of view, it was not intended as such. Rome ordained that its priests and bishops should minister to the people only through structures sanctioned by civil authority, and it agreed to support the civil arm and to inculcate respect for it in the faithful. In return, Rome expected — and received — civil support for its ministry. Taken in isolation, this arrangement might seem effective; however, in Brazil, as in much of the Third World, this grand strategy never succeeded. The problem was that the arrangement did not appear in isolation but was laid inexpertly on top of a history already in place. Knowing why Rome's plan failed helps us understand why liberation theologians remain so wary of pastoral strategies and theologies devised on the Tiber for application on the Amazon.

In 1822, when direct Portuguese rule ended and the Brazilian emperors emerged, nothing much changed in the church. But sixty-five years later, with the establishment of the Brazilian republic in 1889, Brazilian church leaders did have to face a new context. Now, the emperor and his advisors were gone. There were new rulers, the rising business elites and coffee barons who had created the republic, many of them outspoken anti-clericalists and freethinkers. And the bishops had to find a way to deal with them.

The Brazilian situation had already become more volatile with the freeing of slaves in 1888 and with the yearly arrival of many thousands of white immigrants from Europe. Almost all the ex-slaves had been baptized, though the faith they practiced contained a generous allegiance to traditional African elements, rites, and spirits. Catholic saints and black deities melted into each other. The white immigrants came mostly from the lowest and most unlettered levels of the Catholic regions of Europe. There were never enough priests even to begin the vast task of informing these masses of people about the faith. Consequently, by the end of the nineteenth century, the Brazilian church consisted of huge numbers of baptized Catholics who knew next to nothing about Christianity.

Still, a certain kind of folk religion played an important role in the nation's culture. Even before the massive immigrations, most Brazilian farm workers, many of them former slaves, were linked to the landowners by traditional rituals. The workers were very poorly paid, but they were permitted to cultivate (not to own) small plots for their own needs on the same immense plantations where the blacks had formerly lived as slaves and the whites as indentured servants. Since Brazil possessed what appeared to be an endless supply of land, allowing them to work these meager fields was the cheapest and easiest way to compensate the labor force. But the bond between the landowners, who constituted a kind of noble class, and the people who worked the land was not just an economic one. It was also a covenant, a system of mutual responsibilities sanctioned by the rites of the Catholic church. Workers tilled the soil, and in return the landowners provided protection and security in a period plagued by bandits and freebooters. The covenant was sealed through the ritual of godparenthood. At the baptism of a worker's child, the parent would customarily ask someone from the landowner's family to act as godfather. The person asked nearly always agreed, even though the system entailed assuming years of responsibilities not just for the child but for the parents as well. This arrangement created a network of what anthropologists call "ritual kinship." It sanctified the whole system as something resembling a large extended family. Undergirding it all was the local patron saint, who protected and cared for the people in the spiritual sphere, just as the godparent did for the godchild, and just as the landowner himself did on the earthly level. This religiously anchored system was in some ways similar to the thirteenth-century pattern so fondly idealized by European devotees of Christendom. But during the late nineteenth century, it was destroyed, though not by revolution or socialism.

Ironically, Brazil's version of Christendom was destroyed by capitalism, and by the Catholic church itself, as it tried to adjust to a commercial culture and export-oriented market agriculture. Its destruction also was caused by Rome's attempt to build, in Brazil, a Christendom that had not existed in Europe for hundreds of years.

Liberation theologians have no interest in restoring some lost Christendom. Still, they read the history of how Rome actually destroyed something close to Christendom in order to save it as a glaring example of the folly of trying to impose a worldwide pastoral strategy from the Vatican. Of course it was not only the church that subverted the old system. The church had willing allies. The turning point probably came in the mid-nineteenth century with the rise of the coffee barons. These nouveaus came from the chic urban business centers. Though often maintaining the outward forms, they often hated religion and regarded life on the plantations as culturally retarded and superstitious. They were sophisticated cosmopolitans whose eyes were always turned outside Brazil toward Europe, North America, and the world market. Furthermore they did not like tenant farmers. They preferred employees who would not use up valuable land growing their own food and who, if at all possible, could be hauled in just for the single harvest and then sent elsewhere. Nor did they like the inconvenience and obligation of being godparents to a migrant labor force; so religious and ritual ties faded.

Many peasant families would not accept the new conditions.

They refused to work on the burgeoning coffee estates, and, if the lands they lived on were bought for coffee production, they moved away. The coffee growers were often glad to replace them with more recent European immigrants who had no memory of a previous way of doing things. But the need for laborers continued to be intense. Sometimes the tenants did not want to move on, and the disputes between them and the owners became violent. Often the peasants had traditional claims to the land, but no legal title, and when the new owners tried to take possession, the peasants fought back. But the coffee barons had allies in the army and the courts, so the rebellions usually failed. Still, sometimes the confrontations were bloody. In his novel, *The War at the End of the World,* Mario Vargas Llosa gives a fictionalized account of an actual incident in which former slaves and displaced peasants followed a charismatic preacher named "The Counsellor" to the town of Canudos in the wild interior of northeast Brazil and founded an egalitarian Christian city. These impoverished settlers, after successfully fighting off two military expeditions, were eventually defeated by a major campaign of the Brazilian army. All the inhabitants of Canudos were killed, and the city was razed.

The religious appeal of the Counsellor terrified both the bishops and the coffee barons. The churchmen wanted a more disciplined faith, one more responsive to hierarchical direction. The business elites wanted no more spiritual utopians to threaten their profits. Along with their allies in the army and the government, both viewed peasant religion with distaste. The landowners saw it as a barrier to progress, the bishops as a stubborn holdout of pre-Catholic piety. Gradually the two began to see that they might gain more by cooperating than by continuing to argue.

The way this curious alliance took place has become part of the memory of many Brazilian church leaders, and it continues to support their convictions about just how spectacularly wrong Rome can sometimes be in matters affecting Brazil. What happened was that the coffee planters and entrepreneurs became convinced that the religion of the peasants had created a familial style of plantation that made the organization of a mobile labor force impossible. In Brazil, as in many other Third World countries, the capitalist organization of agriculture preceded that of industry, but its pioneers displayed many of the same qualities that appeared in a later generation of industrial tycoons. This new agricultural elite both envied and despised the genteel *noblesse oblige* of the old-fashioned landed aristocracy, and it had only contempt for the ignorance and superstition of the peasants. To shape up the farm workers, a new religious ethic was obviously needed. What should it be?

Positivism, freemasonry, and anticlericalism had always been popular among the European-educated Brazilian elites. But these philosophies had never made much progress among the masses, and only a few secular zealots really believed they could use such liberal ideologies among the zealous miracle seekers who had defended Canudos down to the last man, woman, and child. So that idea was abandoned. They also considered supporting Protestantism, which Baptist and Presbyterian missionaries had introduced into Brazil in the nineteenth century. It had made some headway, but mostly among the middle classes, not among the poor rural folk whom the new elites most wanted to reach. They also knew that the people they needed to touch with a more progressive ideology lived mostly outside the range of schools and the mass media. Many remained illiterate. Clearly the only existing channel available to reach these folk was the Catholic church. But how could that be done?

There had been severe tensions between the church and the new elite dating from the anticlerical tone set by the independence movement that had established the Brazilian Republic in 1889. But now a new opportunity presented itself. Just as the church's leaders needed the support of the new republican governing authorities in order to advance Rome's effort to extend its ecclesial influence in Latin America, so these new elites also needed the church. Perhaps something could be worked out.

Now Rome lent a helping hand. In their effort to work toward the pope's master plan of a "restored Christendom," the Brazilian bishops, along with those of several other Latin American countries, attended a consultation at the Vatican in 1899. The theology promulgated by this "Latin American Plenary Council" came as a welcome relief to the coffee farm owners, though for reasons that Rome might not have foreseen. The bishops who attended the council believed the hegemony of the Catholic church in Latin America was in danger — challenged by Protestants, spiritist cults, and anti-religious secularists. Therefore, the document of the Plenary Council that they brought back from Rome begins by insisting that the Catholic church, and it alone, is the only true way to salvation and that this salvation comes to persons only as they partake in the officially approved sacraments of the one church. Against the idea of predestination, as spread by Protestants, and the practice of seeking help from the departed as taught by spiritists, the Plenary Council emphasized that each individual's eternal destiny depends *on that person alone.* Neither a departed ancestor nor an eternal decree from a Calvinist deity could be relied on. God judged each soul alone.

This insistence on the *individual* nature of salvation is a perfect example of how something that might have sounded good in Rome rang with a different resonance in Brazil. A religiously sanctified individualism provided just what the new entrepreneurs needed in order to wean the peasants from their traditional ties to the old aristocracy and their communal view of faith. They knew that a rural population composed of extended families bound together by godparent bonds, and tied to a village by devotion to a local patron saint, is *not* a mobile work force. It cannot be transported from harvest to harvest, temporarily housed in tents and shacks, and then shipped on to the next plantation. The new agricultural elites preferred a population whose sacral links to the land and to each other had been weakened by religious individualism. They were happy to see the church discourage the lay-led *festas* and patron-saint celebrations, which could not be adequately supervised by priests, since these events only reinforced the customary connections to the village and the patron, which the coffee planters wanted to undercut. Thus did the church hierarchy become an unwitting ally of the rising modern class of anticlerical agribusiness managers.

The social theology of the Plenary Council of 1899 came to its clearest expression in a collective Pastoral Letter issued by all the bishops of Brazil in 1915. It preached something the agricultural elites must have welcomed warmly as just the kind of religion required to keep recalcitrant workers in line. For example, although church leaders had once viewed the authorities of the republic with deep distrust, the Pastoral Letter now instructed priests to "... inculcate the spirit of obedience and submission to those who govern in civil society, in religion and in family ... to lead the faithful to accept their proper situation and the conditions in which they were born and not to hate the modest and difficult life in which Providence has placed them."[1] This meant no more Canudos-type insurrections. The Pastoral Letter also held up the ideal of the Holy Family as an example from which everyone could learn to suffer in this life in order to attain happiness hereafter. More importantly it went on to spell out in considerable detail the obligations which were proper to one's state in life. Thus the faithful were to do their daily work honestly and with deference to those in authority (a Catholic equivalent of the Protestant ethic). It also taught that workers should "respect the conditions of contracts." This is a particularly important phrase. It demonstrates that from the church's perspective the age in which peasants and landowners were bound to each other by sacred tradition and ritual mutuality was over. The church now threw its authority behind the more modern and individualistic notion of the enforcement of contracts. The paradox is that the Brazilian bishops were so eager to follow the lead of Rome they lent their full support to a form of religiosity that encouraged the very individualizing and modernizing currents the same church was so vigorously opposing in Europe.

The question still remained, however: just how was this updated and more economically useful version of religion to be promulgated in a country with the vast size of Brazil? Again, to the good fortune of the coffee barons, who were now being joined by rubber magnates, cattlemen, and other new agricultural interests, the Catholic church would turn out to be helpful in this area as well. A central theme in the papal strategy from the late nineteenth century on was centralization. Everywhere, including in such far-flung provinces as Brazil and other parts of what was then thought of mainly as the colonial world, this strategy called for a tight ship with no loose cannons. In Brazil, however, there were thousands of Catholic fraternities that for three hundred years had been led by laymen; for centuries, numberless processions and pilgrimages had proceeded without clerical leadership. Now the hierarchy disbanded the fraternities (or where possible put priests in charge) and discouraged processions not led by clergy.

The entrepreneurs welcomed the crackdown as a vast improvement. Lay groups and folk fiestas fostered precisely the old-style village religion the new elites wanted to uproot; so, though they were not enthralled by the growth of priestly or papal power, nonetheless they were glad to see the old customs go. Their own worldview was one that appreciated the modern values of education, order, efficiency, and rational organization. The new, more bureaucratic and "romanized" Catholic church of Brazil also spon-

sored these virtues, in contrast to the credulity and irrationality of
traditional village religion. For the church and the entrepreneurs
it was more of a marriage of convenience than a love match. But,
like many such matches, it served its purpose well.[2]

At the level of popular devotions it is also important to recognize how much importations from Europe often served different
purposes when they reached Latin America. By discouraging lay-
controlled patron's feasts and traditional pilgrimages, and by allowing only rites the priests themselves could oversee, the church
used its centralized power to undercut independent local forms of
Catholicism and to impose a more uniform system. The planters
were delighted. They knew that wherever they discovered either a
remnant of the rebellious spirit of Canudos or some leftover local
patron saint's celebration that might keep their workers away from
the fields while they feasted and danced, they could count on the
local priest to deal with it.

Leonardo Boff knows this paradoxical story very well. He also
strongly believes that after nearly a century of clericalization and
romanization, the bold decision of Vatican II to abandon the dream
of restoring a lost Christendom and, instead, to encourage lay ini-
tiatives and base communities was exactly what was needed. Under the old scheme the church had forged alliances with the ruling
elites that needed a religiously indoctrinated and docile work force.
Although many priests and nuns were missionaries who came from
Europe to work among the immigrants, nearly all the bishops —
as in the rest of Latin America — were the social colleagues and
supporters of the rulers and the rich. In return the church got the
support it needed for its spiritual mission.

But after Vatican II and its Latin American follow-up in Medellín, Colombia, in 1968, all that began to change. A new face of
the church as the friend of the poor appeared. Priests and sisters
moved from chic suburbs into slums. The Gospels, rather than the
thirteenth century, became the central model. Priests no longer
worked through existing political rulers but directly in the slums
and the villages with the people's own local organizations. As a
result, when landlords or military regimes cracked down on peasant
leagues or unions or community organizations, some of the bishops
and clergy now supported the people. Letting go the idea that
Catholics should only congregate under priestly direction and steer
clear of secular unions and parties, the church began to encourage

lay-administered base communities and to urge Catholics to join unions, cooperatives, or whatever organizations seemed best suited to protect the rights of the dispossessed. Priests talked less now about devotion to our Lady of Fatima or the Sacred Heart and more about the Jesus who was the friend of sinners and had promised God's Reign to the poor. Out of this new pastoral strategy, which Latin Americans saw as the flowering of the spirit of Vatican II on their soil, liberation theology arose. Boff does not just represent that theology. On a more basic level, he embodies this new "way of being the church" from which the theology grew and which in turn that theology guides.

In Leonardo Boff's Brazil, the elites still think of themselves as supporters of the Catholic church, if not exactly as faithful Catholics. But today they and their clerical allies are the principal domestic opponents of Boff and the millions of Brazilian and Latin American Catholics who share his vision. Though these opponents have little regard for Lorscheiter or Arns, they have their own friends in the Brazilian hierarchy, and in Rome. But they represent a declining wing in the Brazilian church, and they realize that in Brazil, in Latin America, and in most of the Third World, their version of what the church should be and do is losing ground quickly. Perhaps they hope that Rome, as it once did, will come to their aid again.

They may have some grounds for hope from that quarter, but for reasons they can hardly be expected to appreciate. Whatever else motivates the very complicated Cardinal Joseph Ratzinger, it is not the desires of the business leaders of a country far-removed from his beloved Europe. Whatever assistance he might offer in trimming the wings of the Leonardo Boffs of this age will not come because of their importuning, but as the possible by-product of the much more far-reaching vision of the church that inspires him and his supporters, a vision we will now explore more carefully.

9

The Prefect's Citadel

In ordinary governmental bureaucracies, the ten "congregations" that constitute the curia of the Vatican would be called departments, as they are in the United States, or perhaps ministries, or commissariats. As in other governments, each Roman curial congregation carries a particular responsibility, such as foreign policy or education, though, as is the case with their more secular analogs, they sometimes scrap with each other, vie for power, and overlap. Of the ten, eight are located in two massive matching office buildings situated on the Via della Conciliazione, which leads toward the Basilica of St. Peter. One more is in the Piazza di Spagna. The other congregation, the tenth, first organized in 1542 as the Congregation of the Holy Inquisition of Heretical Error, later the Holy Office, and still later, after Vatican II, the Congregation for the Doctrine of the Faith, is a geographical exception. Its headquarters is an old stone palace on a street that, stubbornly refusing recent name changes, is called the Largo Sant'Uffizio. It is close to St. Peter's Square, but not near enough to have been included as a contiguous part of the legally independent Vatican mini-state; consequently, the Lateran treaty, which created that state, made it an extraterritorial possession of the Vatican, like the pope's summer residence at Castel Gandolfo.

I had never been inside the huge iron gate of the Congregation for the Doctrine of the Faith until a cool, clear day in January 1988 when I arrived for a meeting with the prefect in response to his personal invitation, sent me after I had written him that I was coming to Rome and would like to meet him. Although the off-yellow five-story Renaissance palace that houses the congregation has a somber impressiveness, the neighborhood around it seems totally unintimidated. Cars speed by five abreast into

the Largo di Porta Cavalleggeri, oblivious either to the palace itself or to the crumbling stone fountain mounted in its wall whose
inscription states that it was placed there by Pius IX, Pontifex
Maximus, so that both pedestrians and horses could slake their
thirst at its waters. Directly across the street a sign in English
and Italian invites the wayfarer into a cozy cafeteria and snack
bar decorated with old-fashioned posters advertising Coca-Cola
and Moscato Spumato and colored prints of the Colosseum, St.
Peter's, and the Trevi Fountain.

As I entered the office of the congregation, a porter showed
me to a high-ceilinged waiting room furnished with three chairs
covered with thinning brocade and a table whose gold and ivory
paint had begun to chip. Two photo albums devoted to the global
travels of John Paul II lay on the table. The walls were hung with
four paintings — a small one of some cardinal I did not recognize,
one large canvas of a celestial, enthroned Mary, another of equal
size picturing a Mary with her breast pierced by a sword, and a
small one of a smiling John Paul II. A curtained window looks
out on the dome of St. Peter's and the new auditorium for papal
audiences.

After I had waited a few minutes, Cardinal Ratzinger entered
quickly from a side door, welcomed me with a handshake and a
smile, and ushered me into an adjoining room. He was dressed in
a dark cassock trimmed in red and a black skull cap, and he wore a
small pectoral cross. His eyes looked tired, but his manner seemed
hospitable, if a bit brisk.

After exchanging pleasantries, we quickly turned to the subjects
I really wanted to talk with him about — Latin American theology
and how the prefect envisions his role and that of the Vatican
in a world church that is no longer Western. In speaking about
Latin America, it was clear that Ratzinger wanted to speak about
his relations with the bishops, not with the theologians. There
had of course been, he said, some difficulties in the past, but now
communication was much better and the situation was improving.
He said he foresaw a continuing conversation that would eventually
enable the church to take what was best in liberation theology, but
firmly declared that there would be no further official statements
on this issue. He did not seem to want to enlarge on the question
beyond that. He seemed to view the dispute as more or less closed,
or at least he wanted to convey that impression. He added in an

animated way that the Latin Americans had a certain "natural piety" for which he was always grateful.

On the emergence of a world church, the prefect acknowledged that there certainly were unprecedented problems confronting the work his office does. To illustrate this, he offered the example of Africa, which he had recently visited for a series of conversations with the African bishops. He admitted that the bishops themselves were products of a Western formation, but told me that certain questions raised by the inculturation of Christianity in Africa nonetheless were extremely knotty ones. The illustration he gave was the problem of how one was to distinguish the difference between Christian initiatory rites such as baptism and confirmation on the one hand and initiation into the tribe itself, which also carries a certain religious significance. Nevertheless, he was sure that if only the communication could be kept open, these difficulties could be solved.

As he repeatedly returned to the need for communication, it occurred to me to ask what part the silencings of Africans or Latin Americans played in the communicative process. I did not ask, however, and as he continued to talk about a trip he was planning to the United States, it became evident to me that Joseph Ratzinger is a man with an extraordinarily high degree of confidence in his own intellectual and scholarly abilities. He appears to believe that many of the errors he is combating in the modern church are not matters of faith at all but of simple wrongheadedness. Just as his criticisms of liberation theology are not directed so much to the theology itself as to its cultural presuppositions, so also is his disquietude about the misuse of the historical critical method in theology. The problem is not with the method itself, he told me, which in its place can be a useful one, but with its unexamined philosophical presuppositions, of which many of its practitioners are unaware. In listening to Ratzinger, I got the strong impression he believes that if only he and the church leaders and theologians from these various cultures could talk with each other long enough to get the underlying philosophy and cultural presuppositions right, the other problems might take care of themselves.

We had chatted for almost an hour when one of the prefect's staff members knocked on the door to inform him that his next appointment, someone from the Vatican secretary of state's office, was waiting. We shook hands in parting, and the cardinal handed me an autographed copy of a recent book of meditations he had published, mainly on the theme of Easter. The cover picture is taken from an eleventh-century codex now in the Cologne Cathedral. On a red-and-gold background it shows two women both wearing red robes and bearing anointing oils. Their eyes are fixed on an angel with red wings and red hair who sits on top of an open green coffin in which the rolled-up graveclothes can be seen. The angel is blessing the women with his raised right hand. The book is entitled *Seek That Which Is Above*.

As I left Cardinal Ratzinger's office, it occurred to me that none of the paintings I saw on the walls — which might have been hung there by previous occupants in any case — had provided quite the key to the prefect's self-understanding or his role model as the painting of St. Bonaventure in the monastery in Petrópolis had done for Boff. Was there, I asked myself, a saint or a scholar who resides somewhere in Ratzinger's psyche giving him inspiration, as Francis and Bonaventure do for Boff?

Ratzinger himself has at times compared his work with that of St. Charles Borromeo, the sixteenth-century bishop of Milan, who did so much to shape Catholic higher education after the Council of Trent. But that parallel seems insufficient somehow in trying to plumb the prefect's view of himself. I was grateful, therefore, when Eamon Duffy, a member of the Catholic Theological Society of Great Britain, suggested a vivid visual image. In an essay in a special edition on Ratzinger of *New Blackfriars*, Duffy says that when he peruses the cardinal's most recent *oeuvre*, he is carried back to a visit he once paid to a well-known Catholic institution in Toronto in which a huge painting dominated the entire dining-room wall. It depicted, he writes,

> a turbulent sea of blood, through which waded skeletal horses. On their backs, hate-crazed figures in armour raged impotently against a rock which soared into the clouds. On its summit, bathed in celestial light, was a scale model of the basilica of St. Peter's in Rome.[1]

In this painting, which he drolly calls an "edifying example of North American post-impressionism," Duffy finds a splendid insignia for the mentality of *Ecclesia contra mundum*, and he thinks it could easily serve as the Ratzinger coat of arms. It reminds him, he says, of a Victorian hymn:

> Who is she that stands triumphant,
> Rock in strength, upon the Rock,
> Like some city crowned with turrets
> Braving storm and earth-quake shock?
>
> Empires rise and sink like billows
> Vanish and are seen no more;
> Glorious as the star of morning
> She o'erlooks the wild uproar.
>
> Hers the kingdom, hers the sceptre
> Fall ye nations at her feet;
> Hers the truth whose fruit is freedom
> Light her yoke, her burden sweet.

Duffy believes that Ratzinger views the division between the church and the world as a Manichean battle between light and darkness. Outside the church, there is flux and disorder, the sphere where Cardinal Manning warned "teachers may err and therefore mislead." Inside, there is tranquility, constancy, and a changeless fidelity to an inviolate truth. Ratzinger, in Duffy's vision, is the keeper of the citadel.

This portrait may catch one side of the prefect's visage. But it won't quite do. It just isn't subtle enough. It misses a vital something one needs to know in order to discern the issues that separate Ratzinger and his supporters from Boff and his. What brought this talented and dedicated priest to a post we can only assume he finds desirable, but which much of the rest of the world — Catholic and Protestant — finds unenviable? What made him what he is, the man who is perhaps — next to the pope himself — the most powerful single figure in the Catholic church today?

Joseph Ratzinger was born in Marktl am Inn in Bavaria in 1927, the son of a hotel cook and a policeman. He has always claimed that the Roman Catholic faith and culture in which he grew up was all that "immunized" him from the Nazi ideology that surrounded him during his boyhood. Early on, he knew what he wanted and needed to be. "I was convinced — I don't myself know why — that God wanted something from me, something which could be

accomplished only by my becoming a priest." When Ratzinger
tries to recall just what it was that attracted him so powerfully,
he speaks significantly, not first of the attraction of Jesus or of
the teachings of the church, but of the mystery and beauty of the
mass. "The esthetic aspect was so stunning," he recalls, "as it was
the real meeting between God and me." But later on, Ratzinger
says, during his studies for the priesthood, he moved out of the
esthetic into a more intellectual interest in the Catholic church.
"Finally" he says "it became for me, to use a fashionable word,
'existential.' " [2]

Ratzinger was only thirty-five when the Vatican Council assembled in 1962, but he had already gained such a reputation that
the German Cardinal Joseph Frings brought him along to Rome
as a *peritus*, or theological assistant. It was the young priest's
first large-scale theological assignment. At the time, Vatican circles counted on Frings as something of a conservative in contrast
to another German, Cardinal Julius Dopfner of Munich, whom
they viewed as the "progressive." But Ratzinger did not allow
such labels to deter him. He impressed everyone in Rome with
his intelligence and openness, so much so that Hans Küng says
he sometimes cannot believe the Joseph Ratzinger who heads the
Congregation for the Doctrine of the Faith now is the same one
who attended the Council twenty-five years ago.

At the Council, the theological advisor of Dopfner, the "other"
German cardinal, was Karl Rahner, S.J., the man whose person-
centered, anthropological, theological legacy is sometimes claimed
by liberation theologians. Rahner died in 1982, shortly after sign-
ing a letter in support of Gustavo Gutiérrez, who was then under fire from Rome. He is one of the theologians whose influence
Ratzinger and his supporters have sometimes come to regret and
oppose. But in the Rome of 1962 to 1965, the years the Council
continued, Rahner and Ratzinger were friends and co-workers.

In reading today what Küng, Ratzinger, and Rahner said during the Council, it is hard to find indications of the disputes among
them that would eventually emerge. Perhaps the conundrum can
be explained in part by the fact that Küng and Rahner remained
professional theologians, while Ratzinger, although he began his
impressive career as a theological teacher, eventually moved into
the hierarchy. In 1977, twelve years after the Council ended, he
was appointed bishop of his beloved Munich. A few months later,

Pope Paul VI presented him with a red hat. When Cardinal Karol Wojtyla became pope in 1979, he immediately brought Ratzinger, whom he had come to know during the meetings of bishops, to Rome as prefect of the Congregation for the Doctrine of the Faith. Although the new pope made several appointments to satisfy various church constituencies, everyone agrees he selected the bishop of Munich solely because he wanted him. In Rome there is little doubt that Ratzinger is the pope's man.

10

The Ratzinger Report

What makes the confrontation between Joseph Ratzinger and Leonardo Boff important is not just the ideas they defend but the constituencies they represent. The two men embody radically divergent notions of the proper task of the Catholic church in the world, of which theology should inform that task, and even of the nature of Christianity. They also incarnate the growing conflict between the traditional Western (or "Northern") church and the burgeoning Christianity of the previously voiceless outsiders in the Third World. The differences between them are critical, not just because they are so profound, but because they represent the two main options that command any genuine following today, or make any real claim to the future path of Christianity. Of course, there are other candidates. The nostalgic conservatism of Bishop Marcel Lefevre, who once denounced John Paul II as a liberal in an open letter to the *Wall Street Journal,* will continue to simmer. But the Congregation for the Doctrine of the Faith can safely ignore it. Lefevre has no serious theological support, and his following is not growing. American Catholicism may develop its own unique style. But as of now, whether one assays spiritual vigor, intellectual vitality, organizational strength, or popular support, one must conclude that the Christianity of the twenty-first century will either look more like Boff's, or more like Ratzinger's. No other candidates command anything like the intellectual fervor or spiritual momentum that these two do.

This being the case, it is important to underline the fact that Ratzinger is not a "reactionary," nor is Boff a "liberal." Such labels obscure far more than they clarify. Rather, each man represents an alternative answer to the same question: how should Christianity move beyond the twin crises of liberal society and liberal theology? In their highly divergent ways, both men are offering visions of the world and the faith that attribute present sickness of both to the ideas and institutions of liberal modernity. Their deep disagreement becomes all the more complex when we notice that they share a more common diagnosis of the problem than first appears. These remarkable convergences and contrasts become dramatically evident when we compare *The Ratzinger Report,* the book by which the prefect has become so well known, with Boff's *Church: Charism and Power.* Neither Boff nor Ratzinger would have chosen from their extensive lists of published titles the books by which they became recognizable names outside the theological world. For Boff, *Church: Charism and Power* was hardly the work he would have nominated to represent his views in the several different languages into which, largely because of the notoriety Rome lavished on it, this volume has now been translated. As we have seen, it is random, unsystematic, sometimes sketchy, assembled from writings done over a decade. The essays in the collection scarcely add up to the comprehensive ecclesiology a serious theologian would like to be judged on. But it was this text Ratzinger picked as the focus for the controversy. Even though Boff was in a sense the one challenged to the scholarly duel and not the challenger, he was still not allowed, as is customary in an *affaire d'honneur,* to select the weapons.

However, at about the same time Ratzinger made this choice, something quite similar was about to happen to him. In August of 1984, a few days before his colloquy with Boff, the prefect accepted the invitation of an Italian journalist named Vittorio Messori to sit for a series of interviews on the current state of the church. Throughout the interviews, Ratzinger appears to have been remarkably candid. Messori later wrote that he found him ready to let himself be interrupted, capable of laughing heartily, and willing "to answer everything with the most extreme frankness, while allowing the tape recorder to run."[1] The interviews took place over several days at a South Tyrolean city the Italians call "Bressanone," but the Germans call "Brixen." Messori describes it as "the site where prince-bishops once resided, the backdrop of the struggle between popes and emperors, a land — just as it is today — of both friendly and hostile encounter between Latin and German culture." The site for the interviews seems to have been chosen by the cardinal not for its symbolic significance, however, but because it is where he temporarily seeks refuge from Rome's fierce August heat in a modest rented room at the seminary. There he takes his meals in the refectory — simple fare served by Tyrolean nuns — along with other priest-vacationers.

Boff, arriving in Rome just after Messori's interviews with Cardinal Ratzinger had been taped but before they were published, did not know about them. He only learned about them — along with most other people — when in November 1984, shortly after he had returned to Brazil, a Milan-based magazine called *Jesus* published what its editors called a "preview" of some of the liveliest parts of the interviews under the title "Ecco perche la fede e in crisis" ("Here is why the faith is in crisis"). The reaction throughout the world was of shock and incredulity. According to the sneak preview, Ratzinger had assessed the state of the Catholic church since Vatican II in the darkest of tones. He had spoken glumly of a "church in disarray," of "dissension," "self-destruction," and a "progressive process of decadence." He complained that the church was moving along "erroneous paths whose catastrophic consequences are already incontestable." All this, he declared, was due to "the unleashing *within* the church of latent polemical and centrifugal forces"; and *outside* the church it is due to "the confrontation with a cultural revolution in the West...."[2] The people he appeared to blame most for this sorry state of affairs were theologians.

Ratzinger's evaluation was so gloomy many readers thought he had been misquoted or his ideas wrenched out of context. But this turned out not to be the case. When the book itself appeared, first in Italian in early 1985 under the title *Rapporto sulla fede,*[3] it included a paragraph noting that the prefect himself had carefully checked the text. If the cardinal's estimate of the state of the church was a negative one, it was in fact his own assessment, not someone else's.

Soon editions of the interviews appeared in German and other languages. The English edition was entitled *The Ratzinger Report.* The book was read with particularly close scrutiny because Cardinal Ratzinger was then playing an important role in preparing for the "extraordinary" Synod of Bishops scheduled to meet in Rome in December 1985, a meeting some people then feared would try to "roll back the advances of Vatican II." Catholics all over the world were curious about what one of the highest Vatican officials, the head of an organ whose procedures for centuries had been cloaked in secrecy, would have to say in this unprecedented use of the mass media. The bishops who planned to attend the synod read the book in order to find out, if possible, what "Rome's position" at the synod meeting might be.

Fortunately for all these readers, *The Ratzinger Report* is something of a page turner. Taking a leaf from the liberation theologians' notebook, the prefect describes his task as that of guarding the faith, which is a "common good" and a "wealth that belongs to everybody, beginning with the poor."[4] This put everyone on notice immediately: Ratzinger was not going to allow a clique of Latin Americans to corner the "preferential option for the poor." Nor was the prefect hesitant to use straight talk. Take the unpopular word "heresy" for example. He told Messori it is in no sense an outmoded term. Heresy is still present in the church, although today it rarely takes the form of "obstinate denial." Rather, it is more fashionable today to present heretical views by asserting that the official teaching office (the "Magisterium") does not express the faith of the church but only what its antagonists call "the archaic Roman theology." Ratzinger thus makes it clear at the outset of the *Report* that he considers his congregation to be the protector not only of the *integrity* of the faith and of the documents of the Council but also of their *proper interpretation* against cagey theologians who represent "the exact opposite of what is written in clear documents of the Magisterium and claim this is their 'true' meaning." This, he says, is the clever way the new heretics contend that they, and not the congregation or its prefect, represent the authentic meaning of the transmitted faith.

This is tough talk. The *Report* is not one of those dusty theological tomes one puts down with a yawn. It not only demonstrated that the prefect was willing to speak to a wider audience through the press, it also promised to restore to the Catholic world an idiom that had nearly disappeared in the irenic atmosphere of the postconciliar years: polemic.

In *The Ratzinger Report*, there are three areas in which the prefect voices his main disquietude about the church. The first is its exaggerated openness towards those outside. This trend, he fears, has undermined the missionary impetus especially by relying on such glib ideas as the equality of religions and "anonymous Christianity." The second problem is a lamentable decline in the courage of individual bishops, which Ratzinger is afraid stems from the growing influence of national and regional bishops' conferences. By this he presumably means, among others, the Latin American Bishops' Conference, CELAM, which issued the statements at Medellín (1968) and Puebla (1979) on which much liberation theology bases itself. Ratzinger's third major reproof is directed against the sorry decline of strict Catholic moral teaching, which he finds reflected in radical feminism, the continued use of contraception by Catholics despite *Humanae Vitae* (Paul VI's 1968 encyclical, which ruled it out), and the call, especially from North America, for women priests.

For a non-Roman Catholic reader, the view of ecumenical efforts in *The Ratzinger Report* is especially colorful although admittedly its mood is something less than hopeful. The prefect expresses concern that in recent inter-church discussions Catholics have sometimes lost sight of the unique eucharistic authority Christ himself bestowed on their own church's bishops and priests: hence he strongly supports Rome's renewed refusal to allow "intercommunion." He endorses a revitalized veneration of Mary, something Protestants have at times seen as an obstacle to reunion. He also advocates the praying of the Rosary and praises the Lourdes and Fatima movements. He gently refuses, however, to divulge the mysterious "third secret of Fatima" (which he admits he knows, since Sister Lucia, the only survivor of the group of children who saw the apparition, turned it over to John XXIII, who passed it on to Cardinal Ottaviani, Ratzinger's predecessor, for safe deposit in the congregation's archives). He finds much to commend in Catholic "charismatic" movements, but warns that those involved in them should steer clear of meetings with Protestants. He finds the Eastern Orthodox churches "static" and "petrified," and he is afraid that further progress in unity talks between Anglicans and Roman Catholics has been greatly impeded by the Anglicans' acceptance of women priests and the remarriage of divorced persons.

The pace never lags. In one part of the interviews, Ratzinger, apparently speaking in the relaxed mood a Tyrolean vacation spa must encourage, expatiates on evil and the Devil. For the prefect, Satan is not just a symbolic figure with horns, tail, and trident. He is "a puzzling but real presence," a viable force in the world, indeed a superhuman one who works in opposition to God and without whom the atrocities of the modern age are simply not explicable. Further, Ratzinger says, he has noticed evidence of a growing power of the Evil One today in, for example, the return of explicit Satan worship.

In some ways it may be too bad Ratzinger included these remarks about the Devil in the interview. It is not that they are without intellectual merit. Paul Tillich suggested sixty years ago, for example, that the category of "the demonic" should be reinstated in theology; the awesome events of the past half-century do suggest at times that a "merely human" theory of evil is insufficient in the face of Auschwitz, Hiroshima, and the Gulag. Nonetheless, the almost chatty manner in which Ratzinger touched on this profound subject provided a sensational lead-in for headline-writers and overshadowed what he was saying on other subjects. It may even have fed the mistaken myth that depicts Ratzinger as a succubus-chasing throwback to the dark ages. But as his most thoughtful critics know well, this image underestimates the prefect and misreads his worldview.

Ratzinger is a modern theologian. He has read Bonhoeffer and Barth, Kant and Descartes, the Protestant biblical critics, the death-of-God thinkers, the Catholic personalists. He has co-authored two books with Karl Rahner. It is hard to believe he harbors some secret hankering to resurrect the Middle Ages despite the medievalist imagery Eamon Duffy uses to characterize his thinking. He is, in this sense, not a proponent of some "restored Christendom" strategy. Indeed, throughout the *Report,* he explicitly rejects restorationist thinking. The modern world is not all bad, he says. It has produced "certain values that, though they appeared outside the Church, yet, suitably purified and corrected, have their place in its world-view." But he also believes it is sad that many Catholics have fallen into a kind of "conformism" that makes them unwilling to stand up for the real differences their faith requires today, and to oppose what might at first appear to be good, obvious, and logical in the "spirit of the world." But he also tries to be reassuring. Toward the end of the interview, he jokes with Messori about how small his staff is and how poorly paid. This, he offers, ought to be proof enough that they are incapable of carrying out the sort of "purge" their critics fear, even if they wanted to.

The response to *The Ratzinger Report* was largely quite negative. Those who generally support him feared somehow the usually sure-footed cardinal had committed a colossal boner that would make their task and his more difficult. Some even hinted that the pope himself was not terribly pleased about this very public laundering of dirty cassocks. When asked about this, John Paul II guardedly allowed that the prefect was entitled to his own opinions. It was hardly a ringing endorsement.

The prefect's critics, on the other hand, were enraged. Writing in the U.S. Jesuit weekly *America,* Peter Steinfels called the *Report* "an intellectual scandal," which did not "meet a journalist's, let alone a social scientist's minimum standards...." It was "full of exaggeration and gross over-simplification as well as omission."[5] Observers began to speculate on how such a grim evaluation would affect the synod, and despite the reported disclaimers, how close the pope's views really were to the prefect's. All in all the cardinal's jeremiad did not seem to auger well either for the synod, for the future of the Vatican II reforms, or for the approach to theology Boff and his friends were trying to work out.

What surprised those who knew the cardinal best, however, was that anyone should have been surprised by *The Ratzinger Report.* Although expressed in a more popular idiom, it signalled no change in his thinking. A full decade earlier he had already written: "It is incontestable that the last ten years [i.e., since the Council] have been decidedly unfavorable for the Catholic Church." He had complained that "developments after the Council seem to be in striking contrast to the expectations of all, beginning with those of John XXIII and Paul VI."[6] He once responded to Cardinal Julius Dopfner's remark that the postconciliar church was "like a huge construction site" by adding that it was a construction site "where the blueprint has been lost and everyone continues to build according to his taste."[7] But in commenting on the Council, Ratzinger had always skillfully portrayed himself as its stalwart defender against both those on the right who wished to revoke it and those on the left who wanted to leave it behind. In the *Report,* he takes this same position as the Council's champion, but now he concentrates his fire almost entirely on the progressives. This group, he says, now wants to race ahead according to "a presumed 'spirit of the Council' and by so doing they have actually and increasingly discredited it." Ratzinger insists it is utterly essential first of all for all sides to *accept* the Council as authoritative and then to adhere closely to the *letter* of its documents. Here is one case where, at least in the prefect's view, the spirit can kill, and it is the letter that giveth life. But if things are indeed going so badly in the church, two questions naturally arise. What can be done about it? What does Ratzinger himself intend to do?

Ratzinger has the good sense not to keep his readers in the dark about these questions. In the early pages of his *Report,* he says, "As I shall explain in great detail my diagnosis is that we are dealing with an authentic crisis and that it must be treated and cured." What is needed is *not* a "restoration," at least if that means some kind of "turning back." But if by that word is meant "a new balance after all the exaggerations of an indiscriminate openness to the world," then something like it is desirable and necessary. Ratzinger likes to speak in medical metaphors (diagnosis, crisis, treatment, cure). But what is the underlying cause of the disease? In answering the question, it is evident that the former bishop, now a prefect, remains a theologian in that he attaches enormous weight to the role of *ideas:* the cause of the malady is "...that the authentically Catholic meaning of the reality 'Church' is tacitly disappearing, without being expressly rejected."[8]

Both phrases in this sentence are crucial for understanding Ratzinger's diagnosis and the treatment he prescribes (and intends to administer). It is a false "conception" or "model" of the church that is spreading. But the insidious part, he feels, is that the authentic and classical Catholic idea is not "expressly rejected." Herein lies the cunning of the disease germ and the difficulty of the prophylactic.

11

Guardian of Orthodoxy

Life is never easy for the principal public health official charged
with maintaining the salubrity of Catholic orthodoxy. But it becomes even more irksome when the sources of the contagion, the
new-style heretics and schismatics, refuse expressly to reject any
of the doctrines he guards. As becomes clear in the long section
of the *Report* Ratzinger devoted to it, this is what to him is most
frustrating about liberation theology. He writes:

> A theologian who has learned his theology in the classic tra-
> dition and has accepted its spiritual challenge will find it hard
> to realize that an attempt is being made in all seriousness,
> to recast the whole reality in the categories of politico-social
> liberation praxis.[1]

What makes it so difficult for the physician to perform his task, the
cardinal continues, is that "many liberation theologians continue
to use a great deal of the Church's classical ascetical and dogmatic
language while changing its significance."[2] This obviously makes
it the most dangerous kind of heresy imaginable since innocent
people "can gain the impression that everything is the same as
before...." The result is dire: "the very radicality of liberation
theology means that its seriousness is often underestimated." It
"does not fit into any of the accepted categories of heresy." It
is difficult to combat because "its fundamental concern cannot be
detected by the existing range of standard questions."

No wonder the prefect sounds gloomy. The church has con-
tracted a terrible infection, and the diagnosis made by the principal
physician reveals a bacillus that is not subject to any previously
known antidotes. Indeed it cannot even be accurately located,

since previous methods of detection seem useless. At such moments, even a person of Cardinal Ratzinger's sophistication must not be exempt from brief flights of nostalgia. There was a time, before all this confusion, when heretics were easier dealt with. The opinions of the Cathari and the Anabaptists were transparently opposed to the teaching of the Magisterium. Even if some of the methods the cardinal's predecessors sometimes used seem inappropriate today, still the "categories of heresy" were known to everyone, and the "standard questions" were reliable in determining to which category the miscreant should be consigned. From that point on, the work of treating and curing heresy was relatively easy, accomplished either by the Holy Office itself, or with some help from the secular arm. But now a newly resistant virus has appeared. The older cures, even if they were still available, would no longer work to isolate and combat this new deviation. What can be done?

Ratzinger's answer is extremely informative. He says that since liberation theology cannot be effectively challenged at the doctrinal or conceptual level, one must go deeper. He proposes to analyze its "presuppositions," where he feels the real error lurks. It is significant that in undertaking this analysis Ratzinger demonstrates a remarkably acute perception of the clashing worlds of meaning in which liberation theology emerged. Closely following his thinking here helps clarify both where he agrees with his Latin American protagonists and how very deep are the differences that separate them.

The first presupposition of liberation theology Ratzinger uncovers is its suspicion that the classical underpinnings of the received theological tradition would have to be rethought (something Rahner, Lonergan, and some of the French theologians, and the youthful Ratzinger himself, had started even before the Council). So far so good. This might be called liberation theology's intellectual presupposition.

A second presupposition is more social. It is to be found, Ratzinger says, in the contradictions caused by a rich consumer culture in Europe and the U.S. co-existing with the increasing poverty of much of the rest of the globe. Here the prefect demonstrates a fine appreciation of the fact that any theology arises from within a particular milieu. He is correct, and none of the liberation theologians could describe the context of their pastoral strategy and theological agenda better. In this critical situation, Ratzinger goes on, the liberation theologians believe a "new theological and spiritual orientation needs to be sought directly from Scripture and from the signs of the times."[3]

Although perhaps overstated, this is not a wholly inaccurate description. Like many renewal movements in the previous history of Christianity, including the Franciscans and the Reformation, liberation theology and the base communities are rooted in a "return to the Bible." In this case, however, it is a return to the Bible that did not grow up in defiance of Rome but from the renewed emphasis on biblical studies Rome itself had encouraged long before Vatican II. Ratzinger is correct that liberation theology *does* try (using a phrase first introduced into Catholic theology by the French Dominican M. D. Chenu) to "discern the signs of the times." But the prefect is on slippery ground here. The phrase occurs first, of course, in the Gospel of Matthew (16:4) when Jesus urges his disciples to "discern the signs of the times." It was, however, also used by Pope John XXIII in *Humani Salutis*, the document that officially convoked the Vatican Council. What the pope actually said was, "We should make our own Jesus' advice that we should know how to discern 'the signs of the times,' and we seem to see now, in the midst of so much darkness, a few hints which auger well for the fate of the Church and humanity."[4] What did the pope mean? His biographer Peter Hebblethwaite says he wanted "to express his confidence that the Spirit was still at work in the world, that the Spirit acts through the men and women, and through some of the movements of the present age. Salvation is always in the present tense."[5] Ratzinger may well feel uneasy about *how* liberation theologians interpret the signs. But if he is uncomfortable about any theology that tries to deal with the signs of the times, the burden of proof is on him. On this point both the gospel and a recent pope seem to be on the other side.

It is also true that liberation theology, again like nearly all post-conciliar theologies, began exploring alternatives to what Ratzinger somewhat disingenuously calls "*the* existing theological tradition." As the prefect knows, until the imposition of Thomism in the nineteenth century created "the" theological tradition by fiat, there were a number of different traditions and competing schools. One of these, in fact, was the school represented by some of Ratzinger's nineteenth-century German forebears such as Adam Möhler, which

was revived at the Council a hundred years after having been throt-
tled by the Vatican. Another is the brilliant tradition of the French
Jesuits and Dominicans, which was silenced by Rome in the 1950s,
but which also became a dominant voice at the Council.

Professor Ratzinger of Regensburg and Tübingen knows this
history as well as anyone. He also knows that his opponents know
it. By moving his criticism of liberation theology to the level of
its cultural and conceptual presuppositions Ratzinger made the
proper move. But at the same time he may have inadvertently
placed the dispute outside the jurisdiction of his office.

Ratzinger takes a huge step when he concedes that liberation
theology is not in fact a "heresy" at all in any of its standard definitions, that his difficulties are with its "presuppositions." The
problem is that presuppositions are always enmeshed in a particular culture. So liberation theology turns out to be one way — and
there are many others — of interpreting Christianity *from within a
particular cultural milieu.* But the Congregation for the Doctrine
of the Faith is not charged with the responsibility of making judgments about the relative validity of human cultures. The question
then is no longer one of heresy and orthodoxy. Rather it is how
or whether Christianity can become a global faith in a culturally
pluralistic world.

Nicholas Lash, a British Catholic theologian, underlines the
importance of this shift from doctrine to culture. At the close of
the Council in 1965, he recalls, the late Bernard Lonergan, one of
the most respected Catholic theologians of the age, analyzed the
condition of both the church and the world as the result of "the
breakdown of the classical mediation of meaning." This meant,
Lonergan said, that the "crisis" was not one of faith at all but a
"crisis of culture." Lonergan meant that what he called "classical
culture" was passing, and modern culture had taken hold. Therefore theology's task, for Lonergan, was not to try to prop up the
old culture but to begin to interpret Christianity in and to the
new one. The Vatican Council can be understood as the moment
when the Magisterium of the Catholic church officially approved
the undertaking of this task.

In the twenty years that have passed since then, I believe Lonergan has been proved half right. Classical culture does — despite
occasional come-backs — continue to wane. But Lonergan did not
fully understand that what has taken its place is not just some-

thing called "modern culture." Rather it is the eruption into self-consciousness in Asia and Africa and elsewhere of *many* cultures. Few of these have any direct links to the "classical" (Western) culture Lonergan had in mind, and all are wrestling with the enormous power of "modern" culture, especially as it is carried into every hamlet on the wings of an ever-expanding market economy and commodity mentality. Lonergan's crisis of culture has become the crisis of culture*s*.

"A theology," Lonergan once wrote, "mediates between a cultural matrix and the role of religion in that matrix." If this be true, then the cultural heterogeneity of the postmodern world makes theology's task even more difficult than Lonergan envisaged. Theology must not only make Christianity at home in a wide variety of cultures, but it must also recognize that the "Christianity" it interprets already carries the marks of its nearly two-thousand-year-old alliance with classical Western culture, often precisely at the level of those presuppositions that interest Cardinal Ratzinger. Also, the other cultures within which Christianity is now seeking to root itself find themselves in a struggle not only with modernity, which comes from the West, but also with the remnants of the classical Western culture out of which modernity emerged. It is not a simple picture. The Nigerian Christian engineer who read Virgil at Oxford, and who is now trying to affirm his Africanness, must contend with a congeries of cultures within his own psyche. Latin American priests, educated on St. Thomas at the Gregorian University in Rome, but trying to mediate the gospel in the matrix of the exotic fiestas, magic amulets, and the lively remnants of pre-Columbian piety among their continent's poor, are faced with a similar predicament. Compared with the complexity of this job, Lonergan's hope to translate Christian theology from traditional into modern culture seems modest by comparison.

No wonder Cardinal Ratzinger is frustrated by the failure of the normal heresy-detecting methods to function. The issue is immensely more difficult than that of uncovering and eliminating "error." It is how the Catholic church can become "catholic," and so far the Congregation for the Doctrine of the Faith has not given much evidence of its willingness to engage this question very imaginatively. Indeed one wonders — given the previous history of its mandate — whether it is the appropriate organ even to take it on. The Vatican already has secretariats, most of them created by Vatican II, to keep in touch with Jews, with non-Catholic Christians, and with non-believers. Why should the task of helping Catholic theology become globally catholic be left to a congregation whose task in the past has been to uncover and stamp out heterodoxy?

For all his erudition, and even though he occupies a high post in the curia that governs the universal church, Joseph Ratzinger is a European. There is every possibility that an African or a Latin American theologian, even one holding the same position in the Sacred Congregation, might see the question of cultural presuppositions quite differently. If one approaches the increasingly complex issue of the many emerging "inculturated" Christian theologies not principally as a sympathetic advocate but as a sleuth on the lookout for heresy, then the prospect will always be discomfiting. But there is another way.

In the same essay mentioned earlier, Bernard Lonergan said, "Theology consists in conscious reflection upon the message of the gospel in a quite specific situation in terms of history and the human spirit."[6] The prefect's dilemma, one that hardly any of his predecessors have had to face to the same degree, is that the "specific situations" in which theologians now ply this theological task vary enormously. Therefore, the cultural presuppositions — the languages, idioms, overtones, emphases, and tonalities — they bring to their tasks also vary. Unless Catholicism chooses to remain, or return to being, "Roman" in the cultural sense, there is no longer a single normative culture from which the others can be evaluated.

The "world" is not just outside the church as its protagonist and tempter. The world is also inside the church. It is inside not just in the form of heresies new and old, but also as the dazzling variety of cultural matrices within which Christians live. This makes life hard for European theologians, and even Latin American theologians (most of whom were educated in Europe), because they tend to think with the presuppositions of only one culture — until they decide to change. This change, which one Brazilian theologian who was trained in Europe calls "detoxification," is hard enough to go through even when one is living in a new and different environment. To expect this capacity for cultural empathy from Cardinal Ratzinger and his overworked but underpaid staff at the Largo Sant'Uffizio seems too much. The result is confusion. As Eamon Duffy puts it, Ratzinger's fierce rejection of "the world," his call

for a new *fuga saeculi,* is really not that at all. It is not the rejection of the "world" by the church but "the repudiation of one form
of 'worldliness' in favor of another." In a world of many peoples
all created by one God, the future task of theology is a daunting
one. No one culture should be either deified or demonized. All
have their strengths and weaknesses, and in the global megalopolis
there are many "worlds" that have, paradoxically, both very little
and very much in common with each other. Duffy ends his article
with this disclaimer:

> As Christians we bring to the human dilemma, not any bo-
> gus claim to privileged clarities in the hands of irreproach-
> able spokesmen, but the proclamation of a hope for men and
> women *as* they are and *where* they are. The Church *has* a
> treasure; Vatican gilding should not blind us to the fact that
> she holds it in earthen vessels.[7]

Of course, this does not solve the doctor's dilemma. The problem
of deciding what is Christian and what is not, of what the church
should be doing or avoiding does not disappear just because Christianity takes Rahner's leap to a world church. Even if heretics are
no longer subject to an *auto da fe,* distorted versions, indeed ob-
scene caricatures of Christianity persist. The racist theology of
South African Christian nationalists and the consumer pandering
of American TV evangelists merely head a long list. The liberation
theologians not only recognize this, they believe it is part of their
task to expose these and other perversions of the gospel, especially
when they harm those least able to resist them. How to do it?
    Ratzinger would like to solve the problem by trying to make
normative not just the formulation of doctrines, but the cultural
presuppositions that undergird them and *the* theological tradition
to which they gave rise. He does not advocate a restoration of
Christendom in the old sense. What he seems to want is the re-
building, after a period marked by unduly centrifugal forces, not
of a restored Christendom, but perhaps of a new kind of "cultural
Christendom." This would have to include a "recentering" of the
church, intellectually and liturgically, in its ancient homeland. This
is why, in the *Report,* he warmly praises the French hierarchy for
beginning to move back toward a "recentrage." It is why he looks
with suspicion on many of the current efforts to inculturate Chris-

tianity. For example, the prefect is especially wary of those going on in Africa because, as he says, "what is regarded as 'African' may put the common awareness of what is Catholic in the shade."[8]

"To put what is Catholic in the shade": this is the cardinal's underlying fear. He firmly believes that there must be a kind of balancing out of what is Catholic and what is African. The equilibrium must not be lost. But he does not raise the same question about Roman, and especially not about Bavarian, Catholicity. "The Catholicism of my native Bavaria," he says "knew how to provide room for all that was human, both prayer and festivities, penance and joy. A joyful, colorful, human Christianity. . . . I am in no way a 'purist' and have breathed the Baroque atmosphere ever since I was a child."[9]

This is a heartfelt tribute to a "specific matrix." One need not be an *aficionado* of the gentle hyperbole and gold curlicues of Baroque to appreciate its nurturing vitality. But this *Bavarian* inculturation of Christianity might well raise questions in the mind of a Peruvian or a Chinese Christian about whether, at times, what is *Bavarian* may not "put what is Catholic in the shade." In a global church the suspicion can cut both ways.

Nicholas Lash rejects the idea that making a specific culture or *the* theological tradition normative for everyone everywhere is the way to safeguard catholicity and unity. "The unity of the Church," he says "is not only God's gift and promise; its achievement and sustenance are also our continual and onerous responsibility: a responsibility which can only be fruitfully exercised in the measure that *no* group, no sex, no culture, no pattern of discourse, no class (be it clerical or social) arrogates to itself a position of defining centrality."[10]

Must we then have some kind of "cultural Christendom" now that the old political Christendoms are gone? Must the Catholic church, having relinquished obligatory Latin — that immutable and allegedly universal (but dead) language — now impose some cultural equivalent of a single *lingua franca* so that univocality can reign again?

For the liberation theologians the answer is no. What they want is not "recentrage" but "*de*-centrage," a form of catholicity in which the gospel can take root in a variety of disparate cultures and flourish especially among the poor. But this vision understandably worries Cardinal Ratzinger. What would it profit the church, he asks, to gain the whole world, to become global and universal in a sense hardly dreamed of previously, but to lose what he regards as its soul? This is the often unspoken but utterly basic difference that separates Boff from Ratzinger and that informs the alternative visions of the church they pursue. The difference between them, of course, is that Cardinal Ratzinger, as the prefect of the Sacred Congregation for the Doctrine of the Faith, has the authority to criticize and silence. Leonardo Boff, as a Franciscan priest, has only the right "to listen and adhere." He now had the opportunity to express that right, to be silent.

PART THREE

Silencing

12

The Colloquy

On the morning of September 7, Brazilian Independence day, Boff got up early and celebrated a mass in the chapel of the General Curia of the Friars Minor together with the two Brazilian cardinals and his brother Clodovis. Present at the mass also were his sister Lina and another brother who is a professor in Brussels.

At 9:40 a.m., the representatives of the Sacred Office appeared to pick up Boff, who asked once more if he could be accompanied, at least to the outer gate of the Sacred Congregation's headquarters, by the Franciscan minister general. The request was refused. What happened then can best be captured in Boff's own words, which he jotted down later: "I take my courage in my hands and request once again that my brothers in religion [i.e., his fellow Franciscans] be allowed to accompany me in the car. Once again the secretary to Cardinal Ratzinger insists that we stay with the previously established arrangement. I try to lighten the highly charged atmosphere with a little humor. 'It would really be better if they could ride along,' I say. 'That way they can be a part of the modern history of the Sacred Congregation.' I also tried to use a little humor when we arrived — after a fast trip at very high speed through the streets of Rome — in front of an immense gate with an iron grating. To the two men who were accompanying me, who seemed to be feeling both tense and terribly humiliated, I said, 'Aha, is this the torture chamber?' Then we all laughed as we playfully poked each other with our elbows."[1]

Boff was received personally by a smiling Cardinal Ratzinger, his former teacher. Boff greeted him in German. This immediately solved the language question, but it cannot have been easy for Boff to revert to the idiom in which, not too many years earlier, he had been a mere graduate student and Ratzinger "Herr Professor."

After the pleasantries, Boff asked Ratzinger why the papers had
been reporting that he was in Rome on his own initiative and not
at the request of the prefect of the congregation. Ratzinger allowed
that the papers had indeed misunderstood the matter. But then
Boff reminded him that the same information had appeared in
L'Osservatore Romano. Ratzinger did not answer. Instead he
smiled again and indicated with a gesture of his hand that Boff
should be seated at a table. Boff suggested that they begin the
conversation by praying together. Ratzinger agreed. He picked up
a small book from the table and read the "Veni Sancte Spiritus,"
the ancient prayer for the coming of the Holy Spirit.

Ratzinger then offered Boff the opportunity to say or to ask
anything he wished to. Boff started by giving a description of the
current historical situation in Brazil and of the role of the church
within it. He indicated to the prefect how important it was for him
to understand that it was in this particular church and within its
characteristic social setting that he had worked out his theology.
He then went on to select some of the questions Ratzinger had
raised in the six-page letter and to respond to them, consulting
the written notes he had brought along.

The prefect listened carefully. When Boff had finished, he began to ask some questions that the friar later described as focus-
ing on "the relationship between the church of Christ, the Roman
Catholic church, and the other Christian churches." In replying,
Boff referred to the widely heralded change that had taken place
at Vatican II in this area of the Catholic church's teaching. In the
first draft of the constitution on the church, which is known by its
Latin title, *Lumen Gentium,* the text said simply that the church
is (*est*) the Roman Catholic church. The Council however voted
to change that wording, so that the final document now says the
church of Christ "subsists in" (*subsistit in*) the Catholic church.
Boff said that he welcomed this change and saw it as a genuine
milestone in the maturation of Catholic theological thinking about
the church. But he was still puzzled about why Ratzinger was
pressing him on this question since Boff, who lives in Brazil where
there are not all that many Protestants, has actually written very
little on this subject.

In Boff's view, the unity between the church of Christ and
the Catholic church is not something static. It is dynamic. The
church of Christ "realizes itself" in the Catholic church. It comes

to be within the Catholic church to the degree that the institution becomes the sacramental reality it was intended to be and — in its essence — already is. "I do *not* say," Boff insisted, "that the true church of Christ 'does not really exist anywhere' [something he had been accused by his critics of saying]. Rather I believe that the church of Christ does 'subsist' in the Roman Catholic church. But it subsists there 'in the concrete form of promise and of faithfulness.'"[2]

Cardinal Ratzinger was not entirely pleased with Boff's answer or with his reading of the authoritative documents he cited. The best he was able to do on the spot, however, was to disagree with Boff's interpretation of the intention of the Latin words *subsistit in*. He reminded Boff that he, Ratzinger, had actually worked on the Vatican II commission that had produced *Lumen Gentium* and that he was therefore in a better position than Boff to understand what its writers had in mind. What it meant, he said, was best expressed by the word *substantia*, which suggests that the church of Christ both is, and can only be, *fully* present in the Roman Catholic church.

Boff was still not sure why the prefect had turned the colloquy so quickly to this issue. He had simply assumed that Ratzinger shared the general consensus about the Vatican II statement on the church, namely, that it does depart from previous Catholic positions and does recognize a significant degree of ecclesial reality in non-Catholic churches, while continuing to assert that the Roman Catholic church is the only ecclesial body where this reality *can be* present in its fullness. As the conversation unfolded, however, he began to realize that what really seemed to bother Ratzinger was whether one could follow the logic in another direction: if the true church can be present outside the Roman Catholic church, could one also claim that the full essence of the true church is *not* always and everywhere present to the same degree *within* the Roman Catholic church? He was obviously concerned that such an interpretation might indeed be possible if Boff's reading were followed.

Why the fuss over the variant interpretations of one Latin word? Evidently, Ratzinger felt that if Boff's ideas were to be accepted, then some expressions and manifestations of the Roman Catholic church might not be seen as carrying the full presence of the church of Christ. What might those deficient expressions be?

The hierarchy, or parts of it? The content of certain of the papal teachings or those of colleges of bishops? The Sacred Congregation for the Doctrine of the Faith? And if it were granted that the Roman Catholic church is not, or might not be, in all its organs everywhere the full expression of the church of Christ, which "subsists" in it, then who would judge where and where not? For Ratzinger, what might appear to the contemporary reader as an antiquated exercise in straining at canonical gnats seemed rather to be the case of a very dangerous camel's nose pushing under the edge of the Roman tent.

The discussion over the meaning of the word *subsistit* went on for some time. Finally, since they had reached no agreement and nearly two hours had now passed, the difference of opinion was duly registered. But before the two could cover any other subjects, Cardinals Aloísio Lorscheider and Paulo Evaristo Arns appeared — as arranged earlier — accompanied by Bishop Alberto Bovone, another officer of the Sacred Congregation. They had arrived to begin the second and enlarged portion of the "colloquy." (Bishop Ivo Lorscheiter, presumably having decided that Brazil was more than adequately represented, had flown home.)

Cardinal Ratzinger greeted the newcomers and moved everyone to a larger room. He tried to establish a congenial atmosphere, but it soon became clear that Cardinal Arns, who as the bishop of São Paulo presides over the largest Roman Catholic archdiocese in the world, and who has for many years encouraged the church's support of liberation movements on the South American continent, was not in a particularly genial mood. What was on his mind now was no longer just the case of Leonardo Boff but the congregation's newly minted "Instruction on Certain Aspects of the 'Theology of Liberation.'" Why, he asked Ratzinger, in the preparation of this document, had not theologians who had been working in liberation theology for many years been invited or consulted? Why was it written by people who had no actual exposure to the concrete practice of liberation? Further, he wondered why the Vatican had not consulted with those bishops who had over the past years developed an actual pastoral practice with oppressed peoples, thereby providing the context within which the theology itself had emerged? Wouldn't these bishops, he asked, be in a better position to comment on the ecclesial and pastoral dimension of this theological current? Finally, he asked, should not the text itself be written somewhere in the Third World — in Africa or Latin America — in actual contact with the realities it addresses, so that it could be of maximum help to the poor and oppressed people it claims to assist?

Cardinal Ratzinger was apparently not prepared for Cardinal Arns's spirited bill of particulars. The colloquy had not been set up to provide an occasion for the Brazilian bishops to criticize and respond to the Sacred Office's Instruction. It was intended to be an investigation of the theology of Leonardo Boff. Consequently, rather than answer the Brazilians' points, Ratzinger agreed that they had suggested some good ideas and let it go at that. After a bit more conversation he proposed that all those present prepare a communiqué. Its text runs as follows:

> On September 7, 1984, at 10:00 a.m., in the seat of the Sacred Congregation for the Doctrine of the Faith, Father Leonardo Boff, O.F.M., was received by His Eminence Cardinal Joseph Ratzinger, prefect of this office, for a conversation. The cardinal-prefect was accompanied by Mons. J. Mejía. The content of the conversation was provided by a letter which the said Cardinal had sent to Father Boff on May 15 of the same year regarding certain problems arising from his reading of the book *Church: Charism and Power*. To this end, and in view of the previously decided publication of said letter, Father Boff was offered the possibility of clarifying certain aspects of the book which had been indicated and which had created difficulty. The Sacred Congregation, employing its standard methods, will study how to take into consideration in the publication of the said letter the further information which emerged during the conversation. The conversation took place in a fraternal climate. The present communiqué was agreed to by all those present.

All the persons present read the document and signed it. The Brazilian bishops gave Boff a ride back to the Franciscan General Curia.

Boff stayed in Rome a few more days and granted, at last, some of the interviews the various organs of the press had been clamoring for. He taped television programs, later broadcast in Japan, Korea, Finland, Norway, Germany, England, and the United States. In his interviews, Boff frequently said that the presence with him in Rome of two of the Brazilian cardinals had been the most significant part of the colloquy. To him, he added, and he hoped also to Ratzinger, it had demonstrated that whatever else one might say about his own theology and much of the rest of the theology being written in Brazil, it was coming from *within* the church and was designed to serve the church. It was, in a word Boff uses frequently, "ecclesial" theology. He admitted that, in anticipation, the colloquy with Ratzinger had caused him some apprehensiveness. But he said that with his Brazilian church superiors demonstrating such support, it had not only turned out well but might even have set a valuable new precedent concerning how such matters might be handled in the future.

When Boff finally returned to Brazil the following month, he believed that what had first appeared to be a bothersome and unwelcome intervention had turned out to be a kind of blessing in disguise. Before his trip to Rome there were millions of people who had never heard about the church's "preferential option for the poor" (a key notion from the Latin American bishops' famous statement at Medellín in 1968, which they confirmed at Puebla, Mexico, in 1979, and which the liberation theologians have made their Magna Carta). Now, however, they had learned of it through the mass media, which generally ignore such topics. Boff was encouraged and was ready to take up his work where he had left it, and to let the altercation with the Sacred Congregation become a minor footnote in modern church history.

From the Vatican's perspective, however, Rome had not yet spoken and the matter was not yet closed. The *Roma locuta, causa finita est* was still to come. With Boff and the bishops back in Brazil, Cardinal Ratzinger and his staff went over both the written responses Boff had brought to Rome and the oral clarifications he had offered during the colloquy. They finally concluded, however, that despite Boff's good intentions and his repeated assurances of fidelity to the Magisterium of the church, which they recognized, the congregation's reservations about his book "had not been substantially overcome." They decided, therefore, both to inform Boff of this decision and to make public the doctrinal elements in the six-page letter Cardinal Ratzinger had sent him nearly a year earlier.

The letter thus became an official public Notification. It bore the signatures of Cardinal Ratzinger as prefect and Archbishop Alberto Bovone as secretary of the Sacred Congregation for the Doctrine of the Faith. In its final paragraph, it stated that "the supreme pontiff John Paul, in the course of the audience granted to the undersigned prefect, approved the present notification, decided upon in the ordinary meeting of this congregation, and ordered its publication." It was dated March 11, 1985.[3]

Boff of course was disappointed that the Congregation for the Doctrine of the Faith had decided to make public the doctrinal parts of the original letter from Ratzinger, for this is all the Notification consisted of. He was also puzzled about the curious tone of the Notification. Despite all the public clamor, it did not even mention the words "liberation theology." It merely rehearsed Ratzinger's view of what *subsistit in* means. Was it some kind of verbal smokescreen designed to conceal the real debate? Boff had even returned from Rome with the strong impression that since he and the prefect both now recognized the points on which they differed, the somewhat embarrassing public nature of the disagreement — which the Congregation for the Doctrine of the Faith had also found unpleasant — could be ended. But this was obviously not to be the case.

Mainly to reassure himself, Boff now took the time to read through the entire *Acta Synoda,* which is the official version of the decrees of the Vatican Council. He also pored over the transcripts of the discussions of the theologians who formulated the wording. Nowhere, he claims, did he find any suggestion that *subsistit in* was intended to mean *substantia.* He then referred to the final linguistic authority in these matters — the *Totius Latinitatis Lexicon,* which lists twelve possible meanings of the word *subsistere,* none of them close to *substantia.* All in all, Boff believes his research still confirms his contention that the word *subsistit* means something like "to realize in the concrete." Still seeking reassurance, Boff asked Cardinal Aloísio Lorscheider for his opinion. Since Lorscheider had also worked on the Vatican II commission that had produced the document in question, his opinion was an important one. Lorscheider agreed with Boff rather than with Ratzinger.

Boff also recognized that such a public Notification, though certainly nothing trivial, was not nearly as serious as other punishments that might have been meted out. For this he was grateful. The very same Congregation for the Doctrine of the Faith had in recent years barred Hans Küng from training priests or being designated as a "Catholic" theologian. It had also forbidden a French Dominican, Jacques Pohier, to exercise his priestly functions. Compared with these forms of discipline, a mere Notification seemed rather mild. Rome seemed to concur. Joaquín Navarro, the Vatican spokesman who announced the Notification in Rome, strongly emphasized to the world press that the condemnation of some of the ideas of Father Boff was *not* a punishment: "He has not been sanctioned at all," Navarro said, "...there is no threat, hidden or implied."[4] Father Thomas J. Herron, an American priest who works with Cardinal Ratzinger at the Congregation for the Doctrine of the Faith, agreed. He interpreted the Notification as a way to encourage further conversation. It was, he said, intended to stimulate a "healthy dialogue," which had so far been "systematically retarded because of the idea that liberation theology was the way you helped the poor, and nobody could be against the poor." Cardinal Ratzinger had moved, Father Herron added, because he wanted to question whether some aspects of radical thought in liberation theology "were in fact good for the poor at all."

Boff's response to the Notification was in keeping with this publicly stated position of the Vatican that no punishment or sanction was involved and that the Notification was a move to open up a frustrated dialogue. His answer bears absolutely no similarity to the kind of "here I stand" defiance of a Luther. Nor did it convey any of the acerbity of Hans Küng's reply; when the frank Swiss theologian was asked to comment on the matter he said, "The Vatican is, unfortunately, very similar to a lot of totalitarian states that are always demanding human rights abroad but refuse to give them to their own people."

Rather than strike back in any such way Boff chose to submit. "Through this document," he wrote from Brazil on the same day the Notification was published, "the highest doctrinal body of the church has spoken authoritatively. As a Christian, Franciscan friar, and theologian, it is for me to listen and adhere." He pointed out, correctly, that the reservations expressed in the Notification did *not* "qualify my opinions as heretical, schismatic, or impious...." He also reminded his readers that the Notification had not so much as mentioned either Marxism or the theology of liberation. He pointed out that the new problems faced by believers will always demand new efforts by theologians "in communion with the faith of the church community and its pastors." In what sounded like almost an inversion of Luther's *cri du coeur,* Boff summed up his response with the words, "...I prefer to walk with the church rather than to walk alone with my theology."

Everyone, including Boff's severest critics, conceded that his statement was an eloquent and humble one. True, in one sentence he had noted that "the search for truth is an uncoercible need of the human spirit and, even more so, of theology," but hardly anyone could disagree with this sentiment. Again Boff seems to have believed the "symbolic violence" of which he had written years before, and which had now been directed against him, was over. He was grateful, he said that "from the point of view of discipline, the Vatican document anticipates no action against my person and activity." He was thankful he said that his work as a theologian could continue "with serenity and dedication and obviously now with renewed attention to the questions raised."

Leonardo Boff is the only one who can measure his own degree of dedication. But as for serenity, that was unfortunately not in his hands. On May 9, less than two months after the Notification and Boff's submission, another notice arrived from Rome. This one imposed the period of obedient silence. Now at last Rome, in the voice of Cardinal Joseph Ratzinger and the Congregation for the Doctrine of the faith, had spoken. And the Brazilian friar was to be silent.

13

The Silence

Boff had heard rumors that a silencing order might come. When it did, he accepted it without complaint. He told his angry colleagues that he had decided to comply in full, even though he had no idea how long the ban would last. His superiors in the Franciscan order had assured him that silence did not mean muteness. He was allowed to preach homilies at the masses in the little church connected with the monastery, and in other churches, and to teach the handful of Franciscan students who were studying there. Of course he could study, and even write, but only for publication when — and if — the silence was ended. But for the present, he had to forego publishing anything, stop his editing work at Vozes, and avoid all public appearances or contact with the press.

Boff stayed scrupulously within these limits. Although silenced, he was not grounded, so he took a couple of trips. In September 1985, for example, he flew to Managua, to give his personal encouragement to his old friend Miguel d'Escoto, a Maryknoll priest serving as foreign minister of Nicaragua. D'Escoto had undertaken a month-long fast as a plea for peace, and several Latin American Christian leaders including Brazilian Bishop Casaldáliga (the one who wrote the poem for Boff) had come to support him. But while he was in Nicaragua, Boff carefully avoided making any public statements or talking to the press. He restricted himself to delivering a brief homily during a mass celebrated at a small parish church located in a run-down barrio in Managua. The talk was taped, however, and later circulated in mimeographed form. Reading it today sheds some further light on what the friar was thinking during his months of silence.

Boff knew that the little congregation to which he was speaking was closely related to the base communities movement and had been criticized by some ecclesial authorities, including Cardinal Obando y Bravo, the archbishop of Managua. Appropriately, the title of his homily was "A Church Not Built with Stones." Boff told his listeners he, too, had had his problems with churchly superiors. Nevertheless, he compared them and the new kind of church that was emerging elsewhere on the continent to "a little flower in the Amazon jungle that has trees ninety meters high towering over it." But, he assured them, "Everything that has to do with life is strong; the flower has the strength of life." He also added, in words that might have been addressed to himself as well, that although there were people who said they were not a part of the church and had even "wanted to throw you out," still they were "inheritors of the great church of the Apostles" and "in communion with that church."[1] After his brief visit to Managua, Boff returned to the monastery in Petrópolis, to the reading he was doing for the book he was writing on the doctrine of the Trinity, and to his obedient silence.

But while Boff remained in his monastic retreat, others were pressing the case for him and for his cause. In fact the protest against Rome's treatment of Boff had begun even before the colloquy. The publication of the Notification and the imposition of the silencing only intensified it. Already, in August 1984, the international mission center of Boff's own Franciscan order, which is located in Bonn, West Germany, had criticized the campaign against him. The statement spoke of the millions of impoverished Latin Americans whom Franciscan missionaries serve, many of whom find hope in liberation theology and who see Boff as a kind of protector. The document added that no one could possibly doubt Boff's integrity and genuine spirituality. It ended with a plea for a dialogue rather than an investigation.

Brazilian Bishop Adriano Hypolito's response was less measured. Hypolito is also a Franciscan, and his diocese of Nova Iguaçu includes some of the most squalid slums around Rio de Janeiro. He complained that the silencing of Boff "would give great satisfaction to the right-wingers in the Brazilian government and military." He said he considered it the work of rigid and bureaucratically minded people, who could not possibly understand how much Brazil had suffered in the past and continued to suffer from the alliance between church leaders and the elite classes.

The silencing also sharpened the tenor of the conflict over liberation theology. During the fall of 1984 and the spring of 1985, in the period after the first Instruction but before the silencing, both the enemies and the allies of liberation theology had taken advantage of the ambiguity of the Instruction and cited it as a support for their side in the dispute. Boff's old nemesis Cardinal Eugenio de Arauyo Sales, archbishop of Rio de Janeiro, proclaimed "now the battle flag raised against misery and oppression is primarily ours, and not that of the 'liberation' theologians."[2] Boff himself had already hinted how the liberation theologians themselves would respond when he wrote, shortly after the Instruction appeared, that neither he, nor any of his colleagues, recognized themselves in the ideas it condemned. Gustavo Gutiérrez agreed. Whatever the drafters of the Instruction had in mind, he said, it could not be what he and his colleagues were teaching, since they did not teach what it attacked. Bishop Ivo Lorscheiter called it a "rap on the knuckles" and insisted it would not in any way alter what he and his fellow liberationist bishops were doing.

Response to the Instruction from the rest of the world was also mixed: critical, acclamatory, and defiant. President Reagan's recently appointed ambassador to the Vatican, forgetting for the moment his assurances to Congress that the post he held was strictly governmental and had no religious significance, praised the Instruction. He told reporters the administration had become concerned about certain developments in the church in Latin America and that "the time had arrived when the world was interested in hearing what the Vatican had to say on liberation theology." In short, since both sides could cite it and those who didn't like it could ignore it, the Instruction solved nothing. It simply had allowed the differences to be papered over.

With the silencing of Boff, all this changed. Now no one could misread the attitude of Rome, or at least of the Congregation for the Doctrine of the Faith. The adversaries of liberation theology found it hard not to crow. In July 1985, an imposing group of twenty-four critics of the movement gathered in Chile under the leadership of Cardinal López Trujillo of Colombia, who is president of the Latin American Bishops Conference. The group also included the editor of the Latin American edition of the conservative theological journal *Communio,* and priests from Ireland, France, Switzerland, and several Latin American countries. One of the principal participants was Boff's old teacher and critic Bishop

Kloppenburg, who, when he was told earlier of the silencing, had nodded and said, "He had it coming." Professor Anton Rauscher, who is director of the Catholic Center for Social Science in Munich (Ratzinger's home town), gave the principal address. At the close of the consultation the participants issued a "Declaration of the Andes." The statement declares that—however the liberation theologians might deny it—the Instruction was indeed directed specifically against them; that their teachings are incompatible with the Christian faith and out of line with the tradition and social teachings of the church, and they should be rejected.[3]

Meanwhile the pope himself also seemed to harden his position against liberation theology. Passing over Archbishop Arturo Rivera y Damas, the successor of the assassinated Archbishop Oscar Romero in El Salvador, he instead elevated Archbishop Miguel Obando y Bravo of Nicaragua, an outspoken opponent of the liberationists, to cardinal. During his trip to Africa, he expressly warned against liberation theology, often in the same breath with condemnations of a "people's church" not subject to control by the hierarchy. At the same time, the Vatican dispatched curial "apostolic visitations" to check into the work of North American bishops Raymond Hunthausen of Seattle and Walter Sullivan of Richmond. Some people also interpreted Cardinal Ratzinger's attempt to remove Father Charles Curran, a moral theologian at the Catholic University of America, because of his views on birth control and sexual ethics, as a part of the same worldwide crackdown.

But if the *Roma locuta* expressed in Boff's silencing was intended to close the matter in Brazil and Latin America, it did not succeed any better than the Instruction. In fact, it opened the rift even wider between the liberation theologians and the bishops who support them on the one side and their opponents on the other. Some visitors to Rome reported that this had surprised and disappointed the pope. Shortly after the Instruction appeared, it became known that he himself had written the opening, more positive pages in an effort to balance the harsher tone of the rest. He had also insisted that the promise of a second, more affirmative Instruction, be noted in the first. He had wanted Ratzinger's measures to heal, not to exacerbate divisions. But the opposite had happened. Some thought a reason for the pope's perplexity was that he had been led to believe Ratzinger had carefully consulted with the bishops of Latin America, and Brazil in particular, before issuing the Instruction or imposing the silence. But apparently Ratzinger had not.

By spring of 1986, the divisions had become so serious the Brazilian bishops requested that in addition to their individual *ad limina* audiences with the pope, a group of them should fly to Rome to thrash things out. The pope agreed. Some Brazilians began to refer to the coming occasion jokingly as the "summit." Meanwhile, however, further new evidence of the energy of grass-roots Christianity and liberation theology began to appear in Latin America and elsewhere.

It was evident that the movement was spreading rapidly — to the Philippines, Korea, South Africa, and India. In Latin America itself, despite the Notification, the silencing, and the lofty Declaration of the Andes, the tide seemed to be turning. The base communities movement continued to grow, especially in Brazil and Central America. In Chile, Bishop Juan Francisco Fresno, who was thought to be an archconservative and whose promotion to cardinal two years earlier had been cheered by opponents of liberation theology, began to help organize the opposition to General Pinochet's long military rule. In the poor barrios of Santiago, priests and nuns were preparing their people for nonviolent marches and demonstrations. It was in this gathering atmosphere, as Boff continued to sit in the monastery in Petrópolis — named after Peter, the last emperor of Brazil — that twenty-one senior Brazilian bishops arrived in another city of Peter in March 1986. for their long awaited summit meeting with the pope.

14

The Easter Gift

The prospects for the papal "summit" did not seem auspicious to those members of the bitterly divided Brazilian delegation who supported Boff, liberation theology, and a more collegial church. During earlier individual *ad limina* audiences, the pope had read to some of the bishops previously prepared warnings about the dangers of liberation theology. This made them wonder what had happened to the second document on liberation theology, which the pope had promised almost two years before, and which was supposed to emphasize its more positive features. They were afraid it might have been shelved indefinitely. To the summit, the Vatican had invited all Brazilian cardinals, including an eighty-three-year-old retired cardinal and the heads of all the curial departments in Rome. To the supporters of Boff and of liberation theology, this invitation list seemed to tilt the balance of debate in an ominous direction. Some of the bishops feared they were being invited to a replay of Paul VI's famous 1980 audience with the Dutch bishops, after which he had required them to issue a statement that was so "curial" many people back in Holland could not believe their bishops had really accepted it.

Study of the agenda did not make the prospects appear promising either. The Vatican, it seemed, was not only upset about liberation theology, but also about the active role some of the bishops were playing in current programs for land reform. It was concerned about a proposed joint edition of the Bible with Brazilian Protestants. As for the Boff issue, what the Vatican was rumored to have in mind was not an amnesty for him, but a prolongation of the silence that had now already lasted almost a year.

But to the astonishment of the apprehensive bishops, the meeting with the pope turned out to be entirely different from anything they expected. First, John Paul II appeared to be unwilling to take sides between the pro- and anti-liberationists among them. What he wanted, he said, "was an adult dialogue between persons, Christians and pastors." When Cardinal Eugenio Sales, the most outspoken opponent of liberation theology, complained that he felt he was part of a minority that was "getting smaller every day," the pope advised him to repair his relations with the majority of his colleagues. Also, the heads of the curial departments, having obviously been warned by someone, instead of simply telling the bishops what to do, seemed to listen with unusual attention. Finally Cardinal Ratzinger presented a recent draft of the long-awaited second Instruction on liberation theology, earlier versions of which he had already carefully sent in advance. As a Vatican official later said, "the Brazilian bishops were pleasantly surprised."

When the bishops emerged from the meeting, one of them, Luciano Mendes de Almeida, joked with a journalist saying, "No, no, the pope did not pull our ears! Look at my ears. They are white and small and perfect. It was a very brotherly meeting." The pope had obviously chosen to approach the "summit" in a pastoral style, rather than trying to confront the wider theological issues at stake. Nothing was really settled. The statement issued at the close of the meeting was a very general one. The bishops, it said, "have renewed sentiments of gratitude and affection for the pope and full adherence to his teaching and ministry for the Universal Church."[1] Then the Brazilians flew home to prepare for Holy Week and Easter, which were coming up in a few days.

On Holy Saturday, Father Leonardo Boff said mass in a grimy little slum called Favela do Lixo near Petrópolis. The name means "garbage town." When he returned to the monastery, he had just sat down in the common room to relax with his fellow friars when someone called him to the phone. On the line was Father John Vaughn, the same minister general of the Franciscans who had informed him of his silencing eleven months earlier. This time, however, Father Vaughn had a different kind of news. The silence had been lifted. Boff thanked him, raced back to tell the other friars, then returned to the phone to begin calling friends.

Soon the phone began ringing again as newspapers inquired to confirm the report. Now, for the first time in nearly a year, Boff felt free to talk with them. He said he had received the news "as an Easter present" and was sure the cessation of the silencing was a gesture of good will on the part of the Vatican toward the bishops of Brazil who had returned from their meetings with the pope less than two weeks before. "The ending of my silence," he added significantly, "reflects a coherent attitude by Rome in anticipation of this week's new document on Christian freedom and liberation."

The news of Boff's reprieve set off a jubilant celebration among his fellow friars at the Monastery of the Sacred Heart. The following day, at the festive Easter mass, Father Olmiro put aside all restraint and gave way to the irresistible symbolism that the coming together of the feast day and Boff's amnesty inevitably suggested. "In the image of Christ," he told the congregation in his homily, "on Easter, Brother Leonardo is being resurrected on the same day for the church and for his work for the benefit of the poor and the oppressed." But Boff himself carefully abstained from such rhetoric. The minister general had counselled him to assume his normal duties gradually, he said, and he was following that advice. "Rome," he said, had "heard and responded to all the appeals that came from the grassroots and broad sectors of the hierarchy." Whatever he may have felt inside, he carefully avoided giving even an appearance of gloating.

The news came as a great relief to the bishops, both in Brazil and elsewhere, who had supported Boff throughout his long ordeal. They read it as the signal of a different attitude on the part of the Vatican. Cardinal Aloísio Lorscheider, one of the friar's firmest supporters, suggested to Boff that, now that the trial was over, it might be prudent for him to assume a lower profile in his criticisms of how the hierarchy operates. But Bishop Ivo Lorscheiter, Boff's most blunt and outspoken advocate, saw no need to lie low. "The church in Brazil will continue its objective work," he told reporters, "and it hopes that Leonardo Boff will make many constructive and pastoral contributions."

In Rome, Vatican officials again insisted that the timing of the decision to lift the order of penitential silence had not been coordinated with the release of the new document on liberation theology or with anything else. It was, they said, merely a "coincidence" that all these things were happening together. But this time, no one believed them. Boff, his colleagues, the bishops, and nearly everyone in Brazil knew full well that someone in Rome, presumably the pope himself, had wanted the silence lifted before the 400 Brazilian bishops gathered in mid-April for their annual assembly.

The pope knew that the majority of them had strongly opposed the silencing. He also knew that the second Instruction on liberation theology, a draft of which they had already seen at the summit, was scheduled to appear just before their assembly. He hoped the bishops would approve it, and he did not look forward to their coming together still chafing about the punishment of one of their own priests. He wanted the new Instruction to arrive in Brazil while the bishops were still basking in the memory of their unexpectedly favorable "summit" and toasting the new freedom of Leonardo Boff. The timing of the Holy Saturday phone call to Petrópolis was no coincidence.

The eagerly awaited "second" or "positive" Instruction on liberation theology did not appear on schedule. There had been, it seems, some problems with the text. It had been scheduled for publication on Easter Sunday, which fell in 1986 on March 30. About the middle of February, Cardinal Ratzinger submitted to the pope a draft of the overdue document for his approval. But the pontiff did not like it. In the first place, he told the prefect, it was too long and too abstract. He wanted something that would speak to ordinary people. His second objection must have stung the scrupulous and scholarly Cardinal Ratzinger: the way the prefect had used the Bible in the document, the pope suggested, seemed shallow and inadequate. Critics had made similar complaints about the first Instruction, but for the ex-bishop of Cracow to seem to reprove the former German professor for the theological meagerness of his effort cannot have been received easily. Finally the pope, in what must have been a surprise to Ratzinger, told him the document should deal much more positively with the Christian base communities. This suggestion was unexpected, since the pope himself had often spoken very critically about "alternative ecclesial structures" and the popular or "people's" church. So Cardinal Ratzinger went back to the drawing board.

The rewritten document was officially released on April 5, 1986, amidst a flurry of Vatican announcements proclaiming that it was not just about liberation theology but was "a major new presentation of the social doctrine of the church." Entitled "Instruction on Christian Freedom and Liberation," the statement underlined the church's commitment to justice for the poor. But it also drew a sharp line between "spiritual" liberation and "temporal" or "earthly" liberation. It criticized both "police oppression" and the "myth of revolution" but — in line with a long tradition of Catholic social teaching — stated that armed struggle is allowable as a last resort in the case of "prolonged tyranny." It rejected both "individualism" and class warfare. It called the base communities "a source of great hope for the church." There is a nuance of wording, however, that not every reader noticed at once. Instead of "preferential option for the poor," the famous notion from the 1968 Latin American Bishops' Conference in Medellín, this document spoke of a "preferential *love* for the poor." What did this far-from-minor change signify?

Writing in the normally conservative American Catholic newspaper *The National Catholic Register,* Robert Moynihan decoded the difference. "Throughout church history," he wrote, "important theological issues have often pivoted on what appear, outwardly, as minor verbal changes — as in the conflicts over the nature of Christ in the fourth century. Even small changes in the phrasing of historic church documents can have great significance. This document is no exception." The change from *option* for the poor to *love* for the poor, Moynihan goes on, "is an intentional effort on the part of the author, Joseph Ratzinger, to move away from a word with political and sociological connotations, toward a concept with a more traditional religious content. . . ."[2]

The ink was hardly dry on the new document before the argument about its meaning began. The headline writer for the international edition of the *Herald Tribune* put in bold letters what many people thought when he wrote "Pope Using Theme of Liberationists to Blunt Their Movement."[3] Boff himself, however, set quite a different tone for what the liberation theologians themselves would say. He applauded the Vatican for giving a "newly universal dimension" to "values that were initially only those of the Third World." "After this," he said, "liberation theology will gain a new dimension." It was this remark that elicited the puzzled response of one of Cardinal Ratzinger's aides. Boff "must not have read the document," he said, since "I don't see how it can be read to validate the positions of the liberation theologians." Still, Cardinal Arns and most of the other supporting bishops found the new document so surprisingly positive they pushed the Vatican to have the pope himself sign it (rather than just the prefect who had signed the first one). This would have given it the status of an encyclical and made it more authoritative. But the pope contented himself with "approving" it, as he had the previous Instruction. It came, therefore, bearing the signature of Joseph Ratzinger, cardinal-prefect of the Sacred Congregation for the Doctrine of the Faith.

It was in this exultant atmosphere of Boff's release from the silencing, the news of the pope's hospitable reception of their colleagues, and the largely positive response the liberation theologians seemed to be giving the new document, that the Brazilian bishops gathered in São Paulo in late April 1986 for their annual assembly. The meeting had hardly begun when they were greeted with yet another pleasant surprise. Cardinal Bernadin Gantin, who is head of the Congregation for Bishops in Rome and who had come to Brazil for this meeting, stood and read a warm personal letter from John Paul II, written in Portuguese. It strongly endorsed the bishops' work. In words quite similar to the ones Boff had used to describe the universal significance of the new papal document on liberation theology, the pope now told the Brazilian bishops that the theological project being carried out under their care provided "a chance to renovate all of Catholic theology." He concluded by expressing his support for them and for "your dear basic communities," and by asking them to pray for him so that he could become "a true servant of the servants of God." According to one observer, when Cardinal Gantin, who is a black African, finished reading the letter, the bishops were so pleased and touched they rose to their feet and began singing an "alleluia," first just a few, then nearly the entire group. With a mood like this prevailing, not just in Brazil but all over the continent, it was understandable that Gustavo Gutiérrez could say from Peru that "the debate is over."

But had anything really changed? When *Newsweek* magazine looked up Father Italo Coelho, who had conducted the pope on a tour through the destitute *favela* of Morro dos Cabritos during his trip to Brazil, and asked the priest what difference the new document would make, he said, "The document doesn't change anything. We are going to continue to do our same work here."

Boff and his theological colleagues, however, did not appear to agree with Father Coelho. They thought that — at least for the moment — some things *had* changed. If the debate itself was not over, what did seem to be done with was the attempt by Rome to disqualify or silence a theological vision of the future path of the Catholic church that had only seemed to grow stronger under opposition. What Rome seemed to have granted was not a wholesale approval of liberation theology, but its right to be heard, and this is what made the pope's far-reaching suggestion — that the Brazilian church now had an opportunity "to renovate all of Catholic theology" — particularly intriguing. What would such a renovation entail? How would it proceed? Perhaps without fully knowing it, but by appearing to welcome back Leonardo Boff and, by implication, all his colleagues, as full participants in the theological debate about the future of Christianity, John Paul II seemed to be opening more windows than John XXIII did when he convoked the Vatican Council. Sadly, as we shall see, the windows did not stay open long. In little more than a year, Boff was in trouble with Rome again. But even so, it was clear that the theological renovation the pope had called for would now be hard to stop.

Anyone acquainted with Catholic history will recognize something strangely familiar about the hard questions the Boff case brought to light. At one time or another the church has had to face every one of them before: the challenge of *terrae incognitae* and their cultures; popular religious revivals; militant movements among the poor; how to maintain a visible unity in face of it all. Sometimes the leadership of the church has responded deftly and imaginatively. Innocent III's acceptance of the Franciscan movement in the early thirteenth century is a prime example. The decision of the Second Vatican Council to approve the mass in vernacular languages is another. At other times the church's leaders have blundered. The schism of the Eastern church and the Protestant Reformation provide examples of occasions when Rome seemed clumsily determined to pursue the worst possible scenario to its bitter end. Today, the leaders of the Catholic church are confronted by a whole congeries of incipient schisms and potential reformations. This time, however, the fault lines, marking where the fissures could heave open, run not so much along doctrinal lines, but between North and South, between the traditional European center of Christianity and the Third World, and between the parts of the church that are relatively comfortable and the parts that are desperately poor.

Some observers contend that a substantial portion of the Latin American church is already in a state of *de facto* schism, even though an alleluia can be sung in response to a pope's letter and the *de jure* connections with the Vatican are publicly maintained.

Others say it will not be Latin America but Africa, where the inculturation of Christianity has already spawned hundreds of independent churches, that will cause most of the future headaches for the Congregation for the Doctrine of the Faith. The new openness of China, where there is a Catholic church whose bishops were not appointed by the pope but whose Christian population, relying on something very similar to the base communities, has quadrupled in three decades poses another whole set of questions. China is an especially significant case since it is the country where the most imaginative effort ever made to inculturate Christianity — the project of Mateo Ricci and the sixteenth-century Jesuits — failed despite its original high promise mainly because of the short-sightedness of Rome.

Over the centuries, the Catholic church has faced its share of crises. What makes Boff's case so critical, however, is that it seems to contain within itself nearly all the vexing dilemmas the church currently confronts rolled into one. Christianity today is poised on the threshold of the same kind of quantum leap that carried it out of its Palestinian birthplace into the dangerous world of Hellenistic and Byzantine culture. But the world that beckons — and threatens — today is not just the Mediterranean basin. It is the entire globe. What happens next, how the Catholic leadership deals with the multiple issues raised by the Boff case, could shape the contours of Catholicism — and of Christianity as a whole — for centuries to come.

In his surprisingly laudatory letter to the Brazilian bishops, Pope John Paul II spoke of the need for a "renovation of all Catholic theology." I would enlarge that to include all theology, and in the following pages I will draw on the events and ideas that have come to light during the continuing controversy over Leonardo Boff to suggest what that much-needed renovation might entail.

PART   FOUR

The Future of
World Christianity

15

Romans and Brazilians

By the time that the three Brazilian bishops called on Cardinal Ratzinger in early September 1984, the case of Leonardo Boff, which was then being adjudicated, had already assumed greatly enlarged significance. Despite what the bishops told the Italian newspapers, the three did not merely happen to converge on Rome while pursuing their routine activities. They had come to register their displeasure at the way Boff had been treated and to insist that they be present at the colloquy to which their fellow Brazilian priest had been summoned. Of the three bishops, two are members of the College of Cardinals, which is charged with the responsibility of electing the pope. One (Ivo Lorscheiter) is president of the 400-member Bishops Conference of Brazil. Another (Aloísio Lorscheider) is president of the Brazilian Commission on Doctrine, the national equivalent of the congregation Ratzinger heads. The third (Evaristo Arns) is archbishop of São Paulo, the largest Catholic archdiocese in the world. It was lost on no one that these were not ecclesiastical lightweights. With their arrival on the scene, it became evident that the Boff case was no longer yet another dispute between Rome and one more obstreperous theologian, this one from a distant country on the periphery of Christendom.

This case was different. Hans Küng, the best known previous object of the congregation's attention, had received little support from his own bishops. Edward Schillebeeckx had received some. The Peruvian bishops were split down the middle about Gutiérrez. But Boff seemed to have most of the leading lights of the Brazilian church in his corner. Events now began to suggest the genuine possibility of an open breach between Rome and a substantial portion of the hierarchy of Brazil. To make matters worse from Rome's perspective, Brazil is by far the biggest country in Latin America, which in turn represents the largest bloc of Catholics in the Third World. It is, in fact, the largest Catholic country in the world. The place these bishops represented could hardly be viewed any longer, except from a stubbornly Eurocentric perspective, as a "distant country." As we have seen already, a majority of the world's 840 million Catholics already live in Latin America, Africa, and Asia, and the demographic pattern is speeding up. Every day, there are four fewer Christians in Europe and forty more in the Third World. By the year 2000, Europe itself may have to be viewed as "distant," from the vantage point of what will by then be not only the population base, but, if present currents continue, the spiritual and intellectual center of world Christianity as well. The Third World is both the principal source of the various liberation theologies and also the area in which they are spreading most rapidly. When the three Brazilian bishops crossed the threshold of the Congregation for the Doctrine of the Faith that day to demand to be heard, these looming facts of life about the future course of Christianity crossed with them.

Nor is this emergent Third World with its own understanding of the import of the gospel exclusively a matter of numbers and ideas. As the Argentine theologian and historian Enrique Dussel says, it also has a symbolic, even a metaphysical significance in the collective consciousness of the West. There has been much criticism recently of a certain romantic "myth of the Third World," some of it no doubt justified. But certain aspects of the myth seem unwilling to go away, perhaps because the Third World has become the shadow-side of Western culture, its stubborn *doppelgänger*. Quite apart from its own reality, it conveniently represents both the seductive and the terrifying psychic demons the West is reluctant to cope with in its own soul. As the imperial "pomp of yesterday" continues to sink on various dunes and headlands, the Third World also sometimes symbolizes a menacing revenge waiting to pounce. Since Christianity's galloping global expansion in the past 300 years often rode on the wings of Western colonial and commercial ventures, the faith of Third World Christians can be an embarrassing reminder of just how much the cause of God and the church were once used to justify that unsavory enterprise. Hernán Cortés, the conqueror of Mexico, who, despite his shortcomings, had a gift for candor, once said his purpose was "to win souls for Christ and the church, and to get much gold."

Western Christians (or "Northern Christians," as the Latin Americans more often put it) wrestle with these Third World demons as best they can. Sometimes they resort to terrifying images of numberless hordes of barbarians, producing countless babies and threatening the borders of the northern lands with a brown or black or yellow inundation. This is the nightmare promulgated by the right. Meanwhile the left often depicts Third World peoples as the new noble savages, unspoiled innocents who can pour new vigor into our own jaded civilizations. It is this latter idyll that V. S. Naipual takes such visible delight in demolishing. Rarely are the inhabitants of the South appreciated as peoples who, though sometimes vengeful and often just as corrupt as anyone else, want mostly to shape their own cultures and to forge their own interpretations of Christianity without being either demonized or lionized by the North.

When Bishop Lorscheiter and Cardinals Arns and Lorscheider came into Cardinal Ratzinger's office, it was not the first face-off between the emerging voices of the new Third World church and the existing leadership of Eurocentric Christianity. Such encounters had been happening with increasing frequency. But this time it was different for at least three reasons. First, the long arm of Rome had reached out, through one of its most imposing and — historically speaking — least attractive curial organs, to discipline a Third World priest who had won considerable admiration and approval in his own part of the globe. Personified ideas are always more compelling than theoretical ones. In silencing Leonardo Boff, Rome gave liberation theology not only a spokesman, but a hero, almost a martyr. It was no longer merely someone's theories that were at issue. For Latin American Christians it looked like a re-enactment of the Grand Inquisitor and Christ. "They" had silenced "our" Leonardo.

Second, the Boff case seemed different to the Brazilian bishops because they sensed that his interrogation and later silencing signalled something like a Roman vote of "no confidence" in their own leadership. They saw it as a rejection of their whole approach to the church's mission — what they call their "pastoral strategy" — in one of the most impoverished regions of the world. For Bishop Ivo Lorscheiter, whose own northeast region of Brazil is desperately poor, this apparent Roman obtuseness was nothing new. For years he had been encouraging the Christian base communities to take real risks in defending hungry peasants against predatory landlords and a corrupt military government. He has also moved the church, quite literally, into the streets, by himself celebrating masses there and refusing to construct glistening new churches among the dilapidated tarpaper and scrapwood rookeries in which his people live. He has been discreetly cautioned by the Vatican at various times, but he keeps on. "It is difficult for Rome to understand the situation here in Latin America," he says. "We have discovered an underworld, where discrimination and dependence prevail. This institutionalized disrespect of the people is contrary to humanity and to the very principles of Vatican II."[1]

Cardinal Arns, one of Lorscheiter's closest friends, was also alluding to Rome's lack of understanding for his continent when he pointedly asked Cardinal Ratzinger why no liberation theologians had been enlisted by the Congregation for the Doctrine of the Faith to help prepare its Instruction, and why the prefect had not consulted with the bishops who had forged the pastoral strategy out of which liberation theology had risen. These were not easy questions for the prefect to answer, in a church which, on paper at least, is committed to the principles of dialogue and collegiality. The former bishop of Munich was obviously not expecting such queries from three fellow bishops, to two of whom the baffling hand of history had given names just as *echt Deutsch* as his own, but who seemed to speak with a conviction and passion not normally heard these days in smiling and imperturbable Bavaria.

But there is a third reason why the Boff case and the first Instruction escalated the quarrel between Rome and the Third World to a new and ominous level. It is expressed in the final question São Paulo's Cardinal Arns addressed to Ratzinger in the iron-gated palace of the Congregation for the Doctrine of the Faith in the old Largo Sant'Uffizio. Why, he had asked, could the Instruction not be written somewhere in Africa or Latin America, in "actual contact with the realities it addresses, so that it could be of maximum help to the ... people it claims to seek to assist"?

No wonder the prefect offered no response to this last question. Prepare an official document of the Congregation for the Doctrine of the Faith somewhere other than in Rome? In Africa or Latin America? And this suggestion was being made by a member of the College of Cardinals, a man even considered by some as *papabile* in the early hours of the most recent conclave, when it had become clear that a non-Italian pope was possible, but Cardinal Wojtyla had not yet been elected? The idea was shocking enough. Coming from a churchman of Arns's stature and influence it must have appeared close to appalling.

But Joseph Ratzinger is an astute and experienced man. He realized that these bishops were telling him it was now no longer just Leonardo Boff, or even liberation theology, that had come into question. It was their own authority as bishops in their own land. And there was more. By mentioning not simply Brazil, but Latin America and Africa, they were implying a view of church authority that runs counter to everything Cardinal Ratzinger believes. A deep suspicion of national and regional groupings has a long history in Rome. Ratzinger himself once said that in the Nazi Germany of his boyhood it was courageous individual bishops who had stood up to the Nazis. The conference of German bishops at the time, he remembers, was weak in comparison. But his concern dates back even earlier. After the first Vatican Council in 1870 had declared the pope infallible, the next pontiff, Leo XIII, came into office convinced that reducing the regional and national authority of bishops was the first priority. It was a churchly replay of the old story of the king against the nobles. But this time there was no Magna Carta. Leo XIII, having served as a nuncio (papal legate) to a civil government himself, in Belgium, set about centralizing papal authority by strengthening the power of nuncios and reducing that of national colleges of bishops.

Vatican II took the first steps toward reversing this trend. But Cardinal Ratzinger has made no secret of his opinion that the Council went much too far in encouraging collegiality and the mutual responsibility of regional bishops' conferences. He is a convinced advocate of centralized papal power in what he fears is a dangerously division-prone church. He must have recognized in Arns's question that the debate he had touched off could lead to something he very much wanted to avoid: not schism surely — no one had that in mind — but dissension and division, and not just at the theological, but now at the ecclesial level as well. When he thanked the Brazilians for their suggestions but declined to carry the conversation further, he was prudently stepping back from a confrontation he did not intend to pursue, at least not then.

Leonardo Boff also realized that his meeting with Cardinal Ratzinger was more than a personal or even theological quarrel.

As a Brazilian trained in Europe, Boff knew full well that his own evaluation of a century of papal efforts to increase Vatican control differed sharply from Ratzinger's. That may be why he chose to begin the conversation with the prefect by telling him something about the historical situation and present spiritual climate in his own land. It is why he thought it important to describe the pastoral strategy the Brazilian bishops had devised, which is very different from the one Ratzinger favors. He wanted the prefect to understand how his theology and that of his colleagues, far from being a rehash of Marxism, is the product of close cooperation with the bishops in the actual application of their own pastoral plans. He knew that only if the prefect put himself in their position and tried to ponder the gospel from the fetid *favelas* surrounding São Paulo or Rio (or Manila or Nairobi), would he begin to understand what they were doing. In telling Ratzinger about Brazil, he was not describing just one country. As the author of a book called *A fe na periferia do mundo* (Faith on the Periphery of the World), Boff was trying to speak about that whole new world of Catholics and other Christians for whom Europe can no longer be the font of theological truth. But he did it by talking first of all about his own beloved Brazil.

The arrival in Rome of a delegation of Brazilian bishops may have reminded Cardinal Ratzinger that the issues raised by the Boff case are not really all that new. They combine old regional and ethnic tensions, debates about authority in the church, and theological arguments that go back many centuries. But these vexing questions also have more recent antecedents. The fact that two of the Brazilian bishops bear German names may have reminded the very history-conscious prefect that there is a striking similarity between certain elements in the German Catholic thought of the nineteenth century, which was also vigorously opposed by the Vatican, and today's Latin American theology. This parallel has its paradoxical side, since Cardinal Ratzinger, the principal critic of the Latin Americans today, has at times indicated his appreciation of this previous wave of venturesome German Catholic thinking. Recalling some of that history here could provide a useful backdrop to the argument between the Brazilian bishops and the Bavarian prefect and shed some light on the meaning of the Boff case from an unexpected quarter.

16

Two Forerunners

The cool Tyrolean retreat in which Cardinal Ratzinger allowed himself to vent his unbuttoned comments on ecumenicity, Satan, intercommunion, and liberation theology perches on what his interviewer called a place of "friendly and hostile encounters between Latin and German culture." That front has never been a quiet one in the history of Christianity. The "conversion" of the Goths and Ostrogoths often consisted in little more than a priest splashing baptismal waters on a whole village at once. Since the first great missionary to these Teutonic peoples, Ulfilas, was an Arian Christian, the form of Christianity they adopted was not Trinitarian; so theological disputes between Romans and "barbarians" often exacerbated the political ones. Consequently when popes and emperors clashed in later centuries, the line of battle often ran between Latin and German turf.

One such clash came just as the first millennium ended. The papacy stood at a low ebb, and in A.D. 999 the Holy Roman Emperor Otto III (984–1002) decided it badly needed reforming. His solution was to install North European popes, beginning with his cousin Gregory V, and later his teacher, Sylvester I. Both were vigorous and capable men who began to rebuild the papacy, so much so that within a century it had begun to overshadow the imperial power that had instigated its strengthening. The tensions ebbed and flowed but never disappeared. Five centuries after Otto's reform, when the Romans tried to raise the money for St. Peter's basilica by peddling indulgences in the foggy northern provinces, another German, this time a professor from Wittenberg named Dr. Luther, led a protest that grew into the Reformation. From the time of Luther to the present, Italians have had a centuries-long monopoly on the papacy. Before John Paul II, the last non-

Italian was a Dutchman, Hadrian VI, who reigned only one year
(1522–1523). Through it all, the Italians themselves have serenely
continued to believe that what is good for them is — in the long
run — good for the whole church. Still, it must occasionally occur
to Cardinal Joseph Ratzinger, a Bavarian serving a Polish pope,
that this equation has not always been so self-evident to Germans
and other outsiders.

After a millennium of interaction — sometimes peaceful, sometimes not — between the Romans and the northern tribes, Cardinal Ratzinger has definitely crossed the Tiber. It is true that he
serves another non-Italian, the first Polish pope. But just as no
zeal exceeds the zeal of a convert, the Italians know Northerners
who come south often become the most avid Romans. Ratzinger
is an outsider, but he is the pope's man. Still, both his regional
roots and his scholarly familiarity with centuries of conflicts at the
Alpine passages must have given him some added insight, and some
additional discomfort, during the Boff case.

Each generation of popes, it is said, has its own favorite regional nemesis. Pius XII, for example, worried constantly about
the French theologians and the worker-priests. Finally, he quieted
the first with a heavy-handed encyclical, *Humani Generis,* and he
dealt with the second by abolishing the experiment completely.
Paul VI fretted over the Dutch, whose unconventional catechisms
and relaxed ecumenicity seemed threatening. Nowadays, it is the
Latin Americans who seem to be giving the Vatican fits.

Meanwhile, the German church appears to be deeply divided
about liberation theology. Some German Catholics have poured
cash into the support of base communities and catechists. Others
have supported rival Catholic mission groups, who have tried to
tone down the Latin Americans' militancy. But what seems most
ironic about the convoluted altercation between a German prefect
representing a Polish pope and Brazilian bishops of Nordic origin
is that a little over a hundred years ago the theologians who were
causing sleepless nights in Rome were not Brazilians. They were
Germans. Furthermore, their ideas, which were so troubling to
Rome then, bear a striking resemblance to some of the ideas of the
Latin Americans today.

For example, two of Rome's troublesome Germans 150 years
ago were Johann Adam Möhler, who was born in 1796 and died
prematurely at forty-two in 1838, and Ignaz von Döllinger, who was

born three years later but died at ninety-one in 1890. Möhler was a remarkably foresighted, even prescient, theologian. His contribution, like that of his Protestant contemporary, Søren Kierkegaard, was not fully appreciated until a century later. In fact, his early death may have saved him from some of the suffering and exclusion felt by his friend Döllinger, who lived long enough to experience a complete cycle: first one of the celebrated flowers of German Catholic scholarship, then the voice of a persecuted minority, then an object of proscription by Rome, and finally excommunicated at the age of seventy. Still, both men's lives remind us that the roots of the argument between Rome and Latin America and between Leonardo Boff and the Congregation for the Doctrine of the Faith reach far back and that the issues are neither new nor minor.

The stories of Möhler and Döllinger also inject an element of irony that cannot have been wholly absent from the mind of historian-theologian Joseph Ratzinger when he conversed with the Brazilian bishops and with Boff. Möhler and Döllinger represent the German intellectual tradition that nurtured Ratzinger, at least that part of him that feeds on the baroque piety of his Bavarian childhood and the heady days of Vatican II, the big adventure of his young manhood. But Möhler and Döllinger are at the same time the spiritual predecessors of Ratzinger's Latin American antagonists. Like them, they ran into serious difficulties with religious authorities. Eventually Döllinger was completely excluded from the church; Möhler died before his ideas could be either fully appreciated or officially condemned. As Ratzinger pondered what he should do about Boff, he must also have reflected on what the careers of Möhler and Döllinger so clearly demonstrate: that the silencing of a person or the condemnation of an idea — however necessary it might appear at the time — is always a fearful and risky thing to do.

The life and work of Johann Adam Möhler cannot help but call to mind some of the features of recent Latin American theology, for example, its ecumenical vigor, its commitment to cultural diversity, its understanding of history as the place of God's revelation, and its belief in the community rather than the hierarchy as the heart of the church. Möhler pioneered these concerns over a century ago. During the early years of the nineteenth century, when Catholics in Spain and Italy docilely pursued the inflexible scholasticism that was later to be enthroned as the only official theology of the church,

he and some other imaginative German Catholics were building
a whole alternative approach. Historians call it the "Tübingen
school" after the great university where it flourished. The air was
fresh in the Germany of those days. The Grimm brothers published
their *Fairy Tales* in 1812. Beethoven's *Fidelio* was first performed
in 1814, his Ninth Symphony in 1823. The philosophers Hegel and
Schelling were at their prime. The same brisk intellectual currents
that would excite Kierkegaard, Bakunin, Marx, and Burckhardt
were already flowing, and the young Möhler, instead of fleeing
from them, bravely stepped in.

Möhler's early formation was also ecumenical. In 1817, he
was at the Catholic seminary in Ellwagen, when it was moved
to Tübingen to become the partner of the Protestant theological
faculty that was already there. His colleagues and teachers, led
by their dean, Johann Sebastian Drey, made the move enthusiastically, convinced that collegial conversation with Protestant and
secular scholars would be bracing and valuable. Even before that,
Drey had set the example of an open and inquisitive intellectual
style for his colleagues. He kept closely in touch with the Protestant thinkers of his day and with Hegel and the Romantic philosophers, especially Schelling. He encouraged his faculty to try both
to uncover the essence of early Christianity and also to find ways
to build the reality of historical change and development into a
Catholic theology, which he believed still lacked it.[1]

Möhler enthusiastically followed his dean's advice. His early
work, written in the 1820s, is marked both by careful scholarship
and buoyant hopefulness. Influenced by Hegel and the Romantics,
he saw Christianity as a living spirit incarnate in history. He believed that he could sense a revival of religious energy going on
around him, one in which both Catholics and Protestants were
sharing. Reading him today inevitably calls to mind the open and
optimistic spirit that surged through the Catholic church in the
early 1960s and was so well personified by Pope John XXIII.

In his first book, *The Unity of the Church*, Möhler explored a
question very close to one that intrigues Latin Americans today:
the challenge of cultural pluralism. How, he asked, did Christianity
maintain continuity over so many centuries and amid such different cultural climates? For Latin Americans, hardly any theological
issue is more pressing. They know they live in a continent where
Christianity was imposed by conquest. In the Brazil and Mex-

ico of the sixteenth century, whole villages were often baptized in a single day by busy missionaries who had little time to explain what it was all about. As a result, a certain superficiality was inevitable. Consequently, current Latin American church leaders believe it is important to root the faith more deeply in the living cultures of their peoples. Like Möhler, they realize this cannot be accomplished by a top-down imposition but that it must happen, in Möhler's words, as the fruit of "a spirit that forms itself from inside out." In contrast to his Protestant colleagues, who were suspicious of tradition, Möhler obviously delighted in it, but he insisted tradition was not to be confined to the past. He believed rather that it courses through "every period of the church and is alive at every moment."[2] The church not only preserves ancient traditions, it creates new ones.

It is not hard to see that Möhler's understanding of the church comes much closer to that of Leonardo Boff and Bonaventure than it does to the more juridical and hierarchical categories of Cardinal Ratzinger. But by and large his ideas were rejected by the increasingly pro-papal or "ultramontanist" theologians of the nineteenth century, and it took the efforts of a number of determined Catholic thinkers to keep his vision alive in the face of a century of curial criticisms until it eventually surfaced again so spectacularly at Vatican II. Indeed, as the Catholic theologian Thomas O'Meara wrote in 1982 about Möhler's organic image of the church, "It would be a century and a half before Roman Catholicism understood and adopted as its own the theology held in these words."[3] This is certainly true. But it is also important to point out that, despite his vigorous give-and-take with the various philosophies and Protestant theologies of his day, there is something very Catholic about Möhler. Against the nineteenth-century Protestant emphasis on the believer's *personal* religious experience as the starting point of theology, he began with the worshipping *community*. Against the clash of concepts in the World Mind so beloved of Hegel, he focused on real life and actual history. Yves Congar, the theologian most responsible for making Möhler's ideas available to a later generation, says that the main value of his thought is that it demands "an end to the separation between theology and the world and its culture."[4]

One should resist the temptation to exaggerate the similarity between Möhler's ideas and those of Boff and the liberation theologians. True, when O'Meara says of Möhler that he saw the church "not as an archive or a museum but as an organism that is not afraid of history and culture," one that lives "from the Spirit and from the times," the parallels are evident. And when O'Meara continues that, in Möhler's view, "the consciousness of the church belongs not to one or two members but ... is a collective consciousness" that "unfolds in fidelity and in newness God's revelation in Christ," one can see foreshadowed the contrasting theological styles of the prefect and the Franciscan.

But Möhler was no liberation theologian. As Congar, his great champion, concedes, Möhler's theology and that of the Tübingen school were still restricted by an overly narrow notion of a piety lived *within* the church. They lacked Vatican II's robust advocacy of a faith lived in the midst of the secular world outside the sanctuary. In addition, Möhler and his nineteenth-century colleagues were not as concerned as today's liberation theologians are with testing this traditional piety either in the light of the Gospels or by how it worked out in the lives of ordinary people. They wrote long before the great renaissance of Catholic biblical studies and were just not particularly interested in the Bible. Instead they strove to make a good intellectual case for the faith the church had received, and by "the church," Congar points out, they did not normally mean what the people in the pews and the streets had received. They meant what intellectuals and theologians had received. The spectacular Catholic rediscovery of the Bible, and Vatican II's re-emphasis on the central role of lay people, would only come a hundred years later. The liberation theologians believe, on the other hand, that in order to listen for the voice of the Spirit and to watch for what Möhler called the "newness of God's revelation in Christ, unfolding in history," one must pay close attention both to the biblical story and to the actual experience of existing communities of faith, especially of the poor, as they try to respond to that unfolding in the conflict and defeat of ordinary life both within the church and beyond it.

Still, liberation theology can rightly claim Möhler as something of a forefather. He believed the future course of Christianity was in the hands of the Spirit, that unity did not require uniformity, and that the spiritual experience of Catholic people themselves rather than canon law should be the central principle of Christianity. And, like some of the liberation theologians, Möhler also felt the frown of the guardians of another view of church life. The archbishop of Cologne disapproved of his books as too "novel." Troubled by this disapproval, in 1834, he accepted a position at Munich, a university where a century later another original young Catholic theologian, Joseph Ratzinger, was to teach. But Möhler did not survive to fulfill the promise all saw in him. Nor did he live to experience the admonitions, warnings, and silencings that would surely have come if he had continued on the course he set himself. Nevertheless, he appears to have felt the sting of episcopal condemnation keenly. He did not take to such controversy well, especially since he also had to answer spirited criticisms from Protestants while responding to Catholic conservatives. Some believe he was physically and emotionally shaken by all this and that this contributed to his early death. He died of cholera, in Munich, during Holy Week of 1838.

The man who had arranged the professorship for Möhler at Munich was his friend Ignaz von Döllinger, another of Rome's troublesome nineteenth-century Germans. Döllinger was never a member of the "Tübingen school," but his thought also suggests comparisons with that of today's Latin Americans. The son of a humanistically inclined Catholic physician, he blossomed early. By the time he finished gymnasium, he had already learned Italian, Spanish, and English, and went on to master oriental languages and the Greek church fathers. Ordained to the Catholic priesthood, he quickly learned how politics and religion interact by rubbing shoulders with young fellow priests who were protesting Prussian rule over the Catholic Rhineland. His first book, a history of the Eucharist in the first three centuries, immediately won him a faculty position at the University of Munich, a city that was becoming one of the intellectual and cultural crossroads of European life, as scientists, students of mystical writing, and intellectuals from other parts of the continent paraded through it. In Munich, they sipped beer, sought each other out at cafés, and argued the religious and political issues of the day. Döllinger loved the colorful, cosmopolitan city, to which the young Joseph Ratzinger was to come a century later. But unlike the prefect, he never left it.

There was, however, one constant theme in the debates that swirled over Munich at the time, with which Döllinger was definitely not in sympathy: the search for an all-inclusive system. The philosophers and academics of the day were intoxicated by the possibility of some compendious *"Idee"* which would resolve all the manifold contradictions they saw around themselves. But Döllinger preferred facts to theories, and real history to the history of consciousness. As a historian who respected the gritty work historians must do with dusty archives and eroded inscriptions, he was disdainful of those all-encompassing systems that seemed to level down or dissolve the sharp peculiarities of individual cultures and eras. He firmly believed he could serve theology best by helping it come down from the cirrus and dig into the good earth.

Like the liberation theologians, Döllinger combined his scholarly work with active participation in the political and religious life of the nation. He served in the Bavarian state parliament. He frequently acted as a theological adviser to the German bishops. No covert protestantizer, he published a three-volume work on the Reformation in 1848, which was anything but sympathetic. But unlike Ratzinger, and more like Boff and the Brazilian bishops, Döllinger also felt nervous about the growing centralization of papal power. He was especially disquieted by Rome's tendency to insist that all theology should be scholastic. To Döllinger this augured a return to the days when faith was deduced from abstract ideas. It went against everything he held dear both as a Christian and also as a historian who believed that since God had chosen to be revealed in human history, with all its untidiness, history then — both past and present — continued to provide the best place to look for God.

Döllinger's suspicion of inclusive thought systems would surely have commended him to today's liberation theologians, for they frequently point out how provincial such allegedly universal systems always turn out to be. The Latin Americans believe that all theological schemes, scholasticism included, arise because thinkers in particular cultural settings attempt to articulate the meaning of the faith for their times and their places. They have no argument with Aquinas's theology as itself an unusually brilliant example of such an attempt. They differ only with the effort to make Aquinas, or anyone else, however towering, the normative man for all seasons. Consequently, Döllinger's patient insistence on the centrality of history and context resonates with liberation theology. Leonardo Boff chose to devote the first invaluable minutes of his talk with Ratzinger to describing the historical setting within which he does his work. The Brazilian bishops asked why the Instruction had not been prepared in consultation with theologians who were familiar with the actual situation for which it was intended. Döllinger would have understood their point very well.

But once again one must not be misled into premature comparisons. Döllinger was no more a liberation theologian than Möhler was. For him, as it had for Möhler, "history" still had a technical, even academic meaning: it meant the history of piety in the rather specifically churchly sense. For the Latin Americans, on the other hand, "history" means what has happened and is happening to people everywhere. It is the field of clashing contradictions in which theology must work. "History" includes not just dynasties and the careers of the "great ideas," but how landlords deal with peons, how generals organize security brigades, how people cook and dance. Still, the transition from philosophy to history as theology's main focus, a move to which Döllinger made such a formidable contribution a century ago, remains one of the pivotal principles of liberation theology today, and one that brings its proponents into conflict with the present-day successors of the same "Roman school" that once stifled Döllinger.

Döllinger was eventually silenced, and in a much harsher manner than Boff was. Just as today's Latin American theologians labor under the weight of curial surveillance and disapproval, eventually also the German school felt the long arm of papal repression and the censure of the Holy Office. For Döllinger, the real trouble began in 1854, when Pius IX proclaimed the dogma of the Immaculate Conception. Döllinger had no trouble with the doctrine itself. As a historian, he knew it had deep roots in ancient Christian piety, and as a Catholic he personally believed it. What troubled him was that for the first time in history a pope, without consulting a council, had decreed a universal dogma. Döllinger rejected this as an unwarranted innovation and said he suspected the pope's purpose was not just to honor Mary but to solidify the power of the papacy, which he could then exploit for more questionable purposes. He was especially concerned that the new papal authority might be used to impose the scholastic theology of the Roman school as the single one by which all other theologies would then be judged.

Döllinger's suspicions were not unfounded. At the center of the militant legion championing the Roman school and neoscholasticism at the time was a Jesuit named J. Kleutgen, a fellow German. He had been called to Rome in 1851 by Pius IX to work for the Congregation of the Index, which once kept the list of books Catholics were forbidden to read. In the environment of *Romanità*, Kleutgen demonstrated again the fervor of the Teutons who cross the Alps. He turned into an avid member of the Roman school and became a sworn foe of Döllinger and his colleagues. The Dominican historian Mark Schoof quotes Kleutgen as saying about the troublesome Germans, "I want to have nothing more to do with that country or with its confused, yet so inflated minds."[5] One can easily imagine an aide in the Congregation for the Doctrine of the Faith today, perhaps in an unguarded moment, making a similar remark about the Latin Americans, though maybe substituting "stubborn" and "self-righteous" for confused and inflated.

Döllinger thought he saw the gate slamming, and he was right. Papal condemnations of German theologians and scholars multiplied. The pope appointed as seminary rectors only men with clear Romanist sympathies. Döllinger decided something needed to be done, so, in 1863, he convoked an assembly of German theologians, historians, and intellectuals, scholars he believed would appreciate the importance of engaging the ideas of the age. He selected participants who were loyal Roman Catholics but who also respected cultural particularities and would oppose the legislating of a single metaphysics — scholastic or otherwise — on everyone. He fondly hoped the assembly could stake out the grounds for a theology both devout and critical, at once creative and traditional. He was already sixty-five, and he saw it as a last try.

The assembly met in Munich. In a historic address entitled "On the Past and Present in Catholic Theology," Döllinger pleaded with his colleagues to fight for the freedom to do their scholarly work without the intervention of the Roman curia. He said it was time to heal the breach between Catholics and Protestants, and, in this task, Germans who inhabit the land where the split began had a special responsibility. He expressed his doubts that a past age (presumably the thirteenth century) could produce a timeless and transcendent way of thinking. He characterized scholasticism as a "ruin" that itself needed to be replaced.

The speech was eloquent and forceful. But Döllinger received little support. Theologians can sniff which way the wind is blowing, and most are reluctant to take risks. Few supported him. Still, not long after the conference, the archbishop of Munich, Gregor von Scherr — Ratzinger's predecessor seven times removed — received a strongly worded message from Rome about the dangerous theological personages he was harboring. A year later, Pius IX's *Syllabus of Errors* explicitly condemned the idea that scholastic theology was in any respect insufficient. The First Vatican Council was assembled in 1870, but Döllinger, who at seventy-one was the most prominent Catholic historian of theology in Europe, pointedly was not invited. When, after an acrimonious debate, the Council finally approved the idea of papal infallibility, Döllinger saw his worst fears realized. He simply could not accept it. As a man who revered tradition, he insisted the Council had left historic Catholicism behind and had in effect created a new church. Once again the archbishop of Munich heard from Rome, this time in sterner terms. Saddened by what he knew he would have to do, the archbishop procrastinated, but eventually, with great reluctance, he excommunicated the old man who had spent his lifetime serving the church as best he knew how. Eight years later, Döllinger's premonition came true. In the encyclical *Aeterni Patris* of 1879, Pope Leo XIII officially restored the teaching of Thomas Aquinas as obligatory for Catholic higher education in philosophy and theology. Once again, Rome had spoken, and the question was closed.

Döllinger's last twenty years were bleak. He could never bring himself to join the so-called Old Catholic church, which was organized after the First Vatican Council as a protest against what its founders considered unjustified innovations, especially the innovation of papal infallibility. He often considered submitting to Rome, but something within kept him from doing so. He conscientiously abstained from priestly functions, even though Prince Ludwig II thoughtfully retained him as the dean of St. Cajetan's, the royal church of Bavaria, until he died in 1890: a lonely curiosity in the city he loved.

Of Rome's two troublesome Germans, the first, Johann Möhler, died before his ideas could really be put to the test. His theology was granted a posthumous rehabilitation at Vatican II. But the other, Ignaz von Döllinger, lived long enough to taste defeat and expulsion. His principled refusal to submit to what he believed was an arbitrary and unsound decision pushed on the First Vatican Council by Rome resulted not only in his being consigned to the list of theologians one need not consult anymore, but finally in his being excluded from the communion he loved.

The story of Möhler and Döllinger unfolded a full century ago. But if one makes allowances for the differences in detail, it soon becomes clear that the story has much to say about the current struggle between Rome and liberation theology. It tells of the imaginative efforts of theologians who took the particularity of their own cultural and historical situation seriously in their efforts to rethink the meaning of the gospel and the Catholic tradition for their time. It also demonstrates how the understandable attempt of the Catholic church's highest authority to close ranks for the fray can lead to immense personal suffering. It demonstrates a tragic lost opportunity.

But it shows something else as well: how useless it is to foreclose discussions of issues that will eventually have to be faced. A century after they were closed out, the ideas these brilliant and faithful men worked out came to the aid of the church, but only after a great deal of vitality had been lost, due, in some measure, to their exclusion, and after some possibly irreparable damage had been done. There is some element of irony in the fact that Joseph Ratzinger — along with some other present-day German theologians such as Walter Kasper and Hans Küng — is credited with the rehabilitation of Möhler's theology during Vatican Council II. One wonders if Leonardo Boff, Gustavo Gutiérrez, and their colleagues will have to wait a hundred years for their work to be appreciated by their church authorities.

The issue, however, goes beyond whether the church can afford to wait a hundred or so years to cope with today's question. It concerns what the church is. As we shall notice later on, in our discussion of the silencing of women in the early church (1 Cor. 14:33–35), silencing not only denies the full humanity of all who claim to be part of the Body of Christ, but distorts the very language and liturgy by which the church lives its life.

The sad tale of these two nineteenth-century Germans prefigures in its own way what has become the most vexing theological question of the late twentieth century: whether a culturally polycentric Christianity is really possible. Must Catholic Christianity satisfy itself with remaining European, or Western, or even Roman? Is a truly global and culturally variegated articulation of the faith within reach? The Germans were raising all these questions in the nineteenth century. Silencing and shutting them out did not cause the questions to go away. It is hardly possible that when Joseph Ratzinger of Marktl am Inn and of the theological faculty of Munich sat in the presence of Brazilian bishops and theologians bearing good German names, these ghosts of past disputes should not have come into mind.

17

The Marks of the Church

On April 12, 1986, just two weeks after the silencing of Leonardo Boff was officially ended, Cardinal Joseph Ratzinger arrived in Toronto for the second visit of his life to North America. The prefect of the Sacred Congregation for the Doctrine of the Faith was the guest of both Father James McConica, the president of St. Michael's College, which is affiliated with the University of Toronto, and of Cardinal Emmett Carter, the archbishop of Toronto. He was scheduled at the university to speak on "The Church as an Essential Dimension of Theology." This was not a terribly catchy title, but as the time for the lecture drew nearer, it became evident to university officials that the ample hall they had scheduled would not be nearly big enough to hold the crowd. The lecture was moved to the university's hockey arena, which — as it turned out — still could not accommodate the 6000 people who thronged to hear him. The audience listened attentively, sometimes interrupting the hour-long lecture with applause. At the end, they rewarded Cardinal Ratzinger with a standing ovation. Leonardo Boff may have a considerable following. But clearly the prefect is also a man who commands wide support, respect, and admiration in the church.

Paradoxically, in his lecture in Toronto, Ratzinger took a position that Boff also frequently defends — the need for a close link between theology and the church. Both refer to this as theology's essentially "ecclesial" character. "Theology is in and from the church," declared the prefect, "or else it doesn't exist." In words that could easily have been written by Boff, Sobrino, or Gutiérrez, Ratzinger went on: "a church without theology is impoverished and blind; a theology without a church, however, soon dissolves into arbitrary theory." The prefect was talking about

140

something very close to what the Latin Americans call "praxis." They both agree that theology must both grow out of and inform the living community of faith in the real world.

There were other areas of convergence. In answer to a question at the press conference that followed the lecture, the prefect commented on a subject close to the heart of the liberation theologians, the very different "worlds" in which Christianity lives today. Ratzinger said there are three such worlds. In the first world of the West the glut of consumer goods and the pursuit of comfort are leading millions astray. The Latin Americans could not agree more, except perhaps to add that those very consumer goods that deck the tables of the rich "northern" countries are often expropriated from the poor people of their continent. In the "second world" of Soviet hegemony, he went on, Marxist ideology is dead, and a renewal of the Spirit is underway. Liberation theologians on the whole are not very interested in this distant "second world," but when they do speak about it, they generally express themselves in similar terms, and they are particularly pleased with the courageous role the church plays in Poland, whose situation they see as being somewhat similar to their own. As for the third world, though there are many problems, Ratzinger said, "a thriving and genuine popular religiosity may point to a new age for the church." Here the liberation theologians would also agree, though they might have a hard time recognizing the Ratzinger they have come to know as the relentless critic of the base communities and of *religión popular*. Where does all this leave the great debate?

The argument between the friar and the prefect is not about whether theology should be "ecclesial" or about the necessity of the church's learning to live and work in different "worlds." Both agree that the principal task of theology should be to help the church do its work in these worlds. The dispute, however, goes deeper. It is about the very *nature* of that church, and *what* its work in the different worlds should be.

The chronic character of the argument became painfully evident when, in August 1986, four months after the silence ended, the first of the three books Boff had produced during the silence was issued by Editôra Vozes, *A trinidade, a sociedade, e a libertação* (English trans.: *Trinity and Society* (Maryknoll, N.Y.: Orbis Books, 1988) in an edition of three thousand copies. The book was sold out in three days. Immediately the book began to draw criticism from

Boff's antagonists. In it, Boff goes back to the early church fathers and describes the development of the doctrine of the Trinity at the councils of Nicea in 325 and Constantinople in 381. He then goes on to argue that the non-ranked communion and reciprocal mutuality of the three Persons of the Trinity, as defined by these councils, still provides a viable, equalitarian model for the organization of political and economic society today. He also insists that the same democratic structure should inform the organization of the church and that this precludes the possibility of concentrating power in the clergy and the hierarchy.[1]

A few months after the book appeared, the alarm bells sounded again. The cardinal archbishop of Rio de Janeiro, Eugenio Sales, announced through his office of press relations that the diocesan Commission for the Doctrine of the Faith was examining Boff's book and that a document about it would be issued in due time. The person responsible for conducting the investigation, the cardinal's office said, was Boff's old antagonist Bishop Karl Romer, a member of the commission who had the cardinal's full "support and confidence."

Again the Brazilian newspapers sensed a juicy story. They phoned Bishop Romer, but the bishop had learned something from the previous fracas. He was not in agreement, he said, with substantial parts of the text. It was a book that had to be read "with great caution." Accordingly, he was not willing to make public any of his criticisms, and he insisted furthermore that the matter was "far too serious to be treated adequately at the level of a discussion in a newspaper."[2] Since it was precisely the release to a popular newspaper of a critical review by Bonaventura Kloppenburg regarding Boff's earlier book, *Church: Charism and Power,* that had catapulted the previous debate into the public realm, it appeared that this time his critics were being more careful. Even when the *Folha de São Paulo* published some negative remarks about the book a reporter had transcribed from a retreat address given by Bishop Romer, the dispute seemed to go nowhere. When the newspaper asked for his opinion, Boff himself answered testily that the kind of "vigilance" Bishop Romer exercised over Brazilian theologians "did not do anyone any good" and demonstrated a certain "lack of the kind of equilibrium that is important for a bishop and for anyone who speaks about the sacred mysteries of Christianity." Then in a rare lapse from his usual good humor, Boff suggested that maybe what Bishop Romer needed was a "long obedient silence." He added that of course he himself did not believe in such methods of "disqualification and rejection," even though the bishop and his allies had used them in the past and might use them again.[3]

Indeed they might. But it was not the book on the Trinity that troubled Rome most. It was yet another one Boff had also written during his silence, which bears the title *E a Igreja se fez povo* (And the Church Became People). The title is an allusion to the famous words in the first chapter of the Gospel of John, "and the Word became flesh." The book suggests that just as God became a man in Jesus, the church must incarnate itself in people, and in fact is now doing so, especially in the base communities. This book had been forwarded to Ratzinger's office by the same Bishop Karl Romer of the Rio de Janeiro Archdiocesan Commission for the Doctrine of the Faith. In Rome, the prefect immediately appointed a special commission of four theologians to examine it and informed Boff that the commission's findings would be communicated to him through the Brazilian Conference of Bishops. The prospects did not appear promising. Some of his critics were already comparing Boff to Arius, the fourth-century theologian who was ultimately condemned by the Council of Nicea in A.D. 325. His friends were afraid that eventually — like Hans Küng — he might be deprived of his right to be called a "Catholic theologian," which would mean that he would not be allowed to teach in any Catholic theological school, including his beloved seminary in Petrópolis. Even worse, he could be suspended from his priestly functions and not permitted to say mass. This would undercut the pastoral work he does in the village of Lixo near the monastery. Why did *E a Igreja se fez povo* rekindle the conflagration?

The book carries the argument of *Church: Charism and Power* a step further. In it, Boff tells again the story of the phenomenal rise of the Latin American Christian base communities as a new form of the church, reflects on the presence of Christ in these circles of often destitute people from the bottom of society, and argues that these "CEBs" have learned how to represent Christ among the poor more effectively and faithfully than the more traditional forms of the church do. But then Boff asks — and answers — a question that, as we have seen, touches on a matter of great delicacy to the Vatican: which comes first in the church, the community or the hierarchy? Boff's reply is unambiguous: Christ began by founding a community of disciples, all of whom were of poor and humble origin. The hierarchy came later. The church of today should be nothing more than the further development of this community created by Christ on earth. It should be the people of God. But being a "people," Boff goes on to claim, is not a given, not just a fact. It is an accomplishment, something that must be done by human beings. Thus, to help form the poor, who are now no more than a mass, into a genuine people is to continue the work of Christ. Boff documents this thesis by recounting the roles of three personages in church history — St. Francis, Martin Luther, and Alceu Amoroso Lima. But he rejects the idea that a religious leader creates a community. Rather, the leader or priest must be part of the community and should do nothing without its support.

As usual, in making his case, Boff used trenchant expressions here and there, which caught the eyes of those who now scrutinize his every paragraph for evidence of heresy. He often refers to the church, which is constituted by the poor people of the base communities, as the *Igreja popular* (the church of the people). The trouble is that such a church not only infuriates some members of the hierarchy who believe it undercuts their authority, but was explicitly condemned by John Paul II. At another point, Boff says that the church can only claim to be the "people of God" if what he calls the *povo pobre e cristão* (the poor and Christian people) "assume a hegemony in the constitution of the ecclesial community." To some, the word "hegemony" has a clearly Marxist ring, and thus, so they think, Boff must be calling for a kind of class struggle within the church. Even for those who do not give his words such a revolutionary interpretation, what he suggests does not sound like the traditional arrangement, with the priests and bishops on top and the people on the bottom. "After 480 years of silence," Boff says (referring to the nearly five centuries since the European conquest of Latin America and the coming of Christianity), "the oppressed and religious people have finally begun to speak and have broken the monopoly on speech that was once held by the experts in the church: the catechist, the priest, the bishop."[4]

It should have come as a surprise to no one that when these arguments were called to his attention, Cardinal Ratzinger lost no time assembling a panel to pass judgement on Boff's newest work. In the meantime he made sure to prevent the appearance of the books in Italy. He notified Citadella Editrice, an Italian publishing house chartered by the diocese of Assisi, that the book should not be issued in Italian translation and that this should apply also to one co-authored by Leonardo's brother Clodovis with the Baptist theologian Jorge Pixley.

As acrimonious as all this sounds, as we have seen in the previous pages, it is hardly a new debate. It has raged within the Catholic church and in other churches for many centuries. The "friars" of the world, broadly speaking, have always longed for a more fraternal church that expects of all its members a serious commitment to following the way of Jesus, a church that identifies itself closely with the underdogs, that plunges deep into divergent cultures, and that envisions itself as a band of pilgrims celebrating a Mystery that already suffuses the world. The "prefects" prefer a more hierarchically ordered church that mediates Grace from heaven to earth, that relies on alliances with those who already bear the discipline and responsibility of power, and that bases itself primarily in the culture the church has already nourished for centuries.

This argument about what the church is and what it should be doing today echoes the very old controversy over what have traditionally been known as the four "marks of the church," the so-called *notae ecclesiae*. The "true" church, according to the historic creeds, must be *one, holy, catholic,* and *apostolic*. The rule of thumb is that where these marks can be discerned, there the true church of Jesus Christ exists, but that where one or more of the marks is missing the church is not truly present. Something essential to the church is missing. Neither side in the present debate disputes this ancient rule; but the argument between Ratzinger and Boff opens the old discussion about the marks of the church again.

The clamor over the silencing itself receded quickly after the Vatican ended it in March 1986. But ensuing events demonstrated that the divisive issues brought up by the Boff case remained. The disputes he had stirred up about the relationship of the hierarchy to grassroots religious communities, the place of the poor in the church, and the challenge of religious and cultural diversity had not been resolved. Furthermore it had also become clear that each of these issues leads back to an even more fundamental one about the historic marks of the church:

1. The assertion by liberation theology that fidelity to the message of Jesus requires a partisan option for the poor constitutes a claim about *apostolicity,* the nature of the connection between today's church and its origins.

2. The vexed problem of how the institutional churches' leadership should deal with *religión popular,* internal dissent, and the volatile new religious movements springing up from the grassroots — such as the Christian base communities — raises the question of the church's *holiness,* its ability to exemplify in its own life what it is teaching the world.

3. The emergence in recent decades of a culturally pluralistic world church with a non-Western majority poses the mystery of the church's *catholicity,* its universal inclusiveness, in a particularly sharp way.

4. Finally, the problem of how the church can remain in some real sense a single church despite all this tension, conflict, and diversity is clearly a matter of its mark of *oneness.*

Thus, we find ourselves in the midst of a new debate about an old subject: the marks of the church. Will it ever be possible for the two major parties in today's controversy to agree on what the historic marks of the church should be in this radically altered environment of the late twentieth century? This question is an urgent one because it concerns something both the friars and the prefects believe is essential: norms. It has to do with making the difficult but necessary judgements about what the church should be doing and what it ought to be teaching, about what is authentically Christian and what is not. Sometimes Cardinal Ratzinger's supporters claim that he recognizes the hard necessity of making such choices better than the liberation theologians do, that they advocate a view of Christianity which — even if they do not intend it — could easily lead to anarchy and anomie, a church where anything goes. But this is actually not the case. Both the liberation theologians and the supporters of Cardinal Ratzinger agree that the church has strayed from the narrow path Christ marked out and that it needs discipline, a term derived from the same root the word "disciple" comes from. But they differ on what this discipline should be. For Ratzinger, as we have seen, the church's present flaccidness is traceable to its excessive accommodations to the modern world and its mistaken interpretations of an alleged "spirit of the Council." The tightening up he wants will require, therefore, a "recentrage," a reassertion of firm papal authority, a slowing down of ecumenical momentum, a renewed emphasis on what is Roman about the Catholic church.

Even some liberation theologians trace at least part of the flabbiness back to Vatican II, but in a different way. Jon Sobrino writes that he once warmly welcomed the Council's shift in imagery about the church from "body of Christ" to "people of God." He saw it as an appropriate expression of the Council's distrust of elitism (a church centered on the hierarchy and the priesthood). But he has come to believe, he says, that it turned out to be a mistake for the Council and its interpreters to underscore so much the "all" who constitute the people of God. Though this "all" had a certain positive democratizing value, at the time, he says, it soon misled people into thinking of the church as "universal in a vague sort of way." Sobrino fears this vague universalism allows too much slippage and can even be read to imply that the church need not demand much from its members. Like Ratzinger, both Boff and Sobrino want the church to be more disciplined, not less. What is at issue between the two parties is not *whether* there should be norms and discipline but *what* they should be.

The "friaral" view of the church and the "prefectural" one move in different ways to answer this question. Are their differences unresolvable? I believe the divergences between these two approaches are deep and serious. I also believe, however, that by examining how each side looks at the four historic marks as they re-emerge in the central questions raised by the Boff case (the role of the poor, *religión popular,* cultural pluralism, and church unity), it becomes possible to sort out the differences between the parties. Having done this we can then go on to distinguish between those issues on which some consensus might appear, and those on which, since there seems little likelihood of an agreement very soon, the primordial litigation between the friars and the prefects will probably continue for a long time to come.

In the final pages of this book, we will examine each of the marks in detail and explore the ramifications of the debate each is undergoing in a time of conflict between Rome and liberation theology.

18

Apostolicity and the Poor

Apostolicity is the mark of the church that refers to its continuity with Christ and the apostles. Both sides in the Boff dispute agree that apostolicity is an essential quality of the Christian church. But what does it mean for the church to be apostolic today, and what does apostolicity have to do with the "preferential option for the poor" or with becoming what John XXIII called for: a "church *of* the poor"? Here is where the disagreement sets in.

For most conventional Catholic theologians, the litmus test of apostolicity is to ascertain whether any claimant to Christian identity today can demonstrate *visible institutional continuity* with the apostles of Christ and their present-day successors, the pope and the bishops. For Boff and the friars on the other hand, apostolicity means faithfully *continuing the work* and *ministry* Christ and his apostles actually did, and this obviously entails, as it did for them, a preference for the outcasts. To be truly apostolic for Boff requires taking the side of the poor — whether one calls this "love" or "option." It is the gospel itself that requires the preference. And where this mark is missing, where the church remains neutral or allies itself with the powerful, one is justified in harboring at least some doubts about its genuine apostolicity.

Can the dispute over this norm ever be settled? *The Modern Catholic Dictionary* states that the word "apostles" refers to the "followers of Jesus who spread his message." During Jesus' own lifetime, the entry continues, these men are referred to as "disciples," but "following his ascension they are always called apostles."[1] "Apostolicity," then, refers to two aspects of the church. The first is its origin in the life and ministry of Jesus and his followers. The second has to do with its "mission," its *being sent* by God to do something in the world. The Greek word *apostolos*

149

actually means someone who is sent to do some task. In order to grasp the import of the difference between Boff and Ratzinger and their respective supporters on this point we must first ask how they envision the church's link to Jesus; and we must then find out how they believe this link should be expressed in its apostolate, its "sent-ness" today.

The difference between the friars and the prefects on these issues can be evoked in one question: how much continuity is there between a "disciple," one who seeks to follow Jesus, and an "apostle," one who carries the gospel to the world? Another way to put the question is this: how much should the earthly life of the Jesus of the Gospels shape the current life of the church nineteen centuries later? In other words, how much does "representing" Jesus today (apostolicity) entail "following" him (discipleship)?

The answer to this question is that for the liberation theologians there is a great deal of continuity between the historical Jesus of the Gospels and the task of the church today, and therefore between discipleship and apostolicity, between following and representing. For the other side in the debate, there is not only much less continuity between Jesus and the early church, there is in fact a great gulf. The mission of the church begins not with the disciples but with those who met the Risen Christ, the apostles. Easter changed everything. Therefore, the church should *not* be traced back to the historical Jesus. Properly speaking it begins only after the Resurrection of Christ, and its mission is not so much to "follow Jesus" but to represent Christ, not to be disciples but to be apostles.

The argument about whether the church arose mainly out of the events of Jesus' earthly life or mainly out of subsequent events can often become a tangled thicket. It also sometimes takes surprising turns. A century ago, it was the strict papalists who insisted that Christ himself had founded the church-hierarchy, pope and all — and it was the so-called modernist Catholic scholars who raised questions about whether Jesus ever really intended to found a church at all. One of the modernists' main spokesmen, Alfred Loisy, was criticized in 1903 by Cardinal Richard of Paris for voicing this reservation. Loisy's ideas were soon condemned by the Holy Office (the congregation Ratzinger now heads) in *Lamentabili* in 1907.

The prefect has written a lot on the question of whether the historical Jesus actually founded the church, but his views are not entirely consistent. Sometimes he seems to trace its founding back to Jesus' calling of the "Twelve." This would mean, of course, that the church began with what eventually became the hierarchy, a theory that gives the hierarchy both historical and religious priority over the "people of God." But in other places, following the earlier work of Erik Peterson, he argues that the church does not exist because it was directly willed by Christ. It exists, rather, because when his own people, the Jews, did not accept his message, and the expected Kingdom failed to come right away, the apostles — inspired by the Risen Christ — turned to the Gentiles who then constituted the church and became the "new people of God."[2]

Sometimes the debate comes down to the question of just *how much* of a "great divide" does the first Easter morning represent? Both sides believe in the Resurrection of Jesus Christ. What the liberation theologians continually point out, however, is that it is the *same* Jesus of the Gospels, the Sermon on the Mount, and the confrontation with Pilate and the ruling elites of Jerusalem who was raised on Easter Sunday. Therefore they insist the Risen Christ *includes* the historical Jesus, and apostolicity must *include* discipleship. Jon Sobrino puts it this way:

> The risen Lord who brings a community into existence is not just any human being nor any Christ but the crucified Jesus of Nazareth. Consequently ... the Church absorbed into its faith ... those things in the life of Jesus that led to the cross and resurrection ... his ministry to the poor, his solidarity with them, his compassion on the multitudes, his attacks on the mighty, and his condemnation and execution by them. I may state as a *theological* thesis that according to the New Testament the Church certainly *arises* because of the resurrection, but also that *that which* arises is in conformity with ... a concrete life of solidarity with the poor and of service to them.[3]

This means that for Sobrino (and most of the other liberation theologians) one simply cannot represent Christ today without also following him. Apostolicity entails discipleship. Ratzinger and his school of interpreters generally deny that there is or should be a strong element of continuity between the actions of the historical

Jesus and his followers on the one side, and the nature and task of the church today on the other. Almost inverting the terms of the old modernist debate, they criticize the liberation theologians for underlining the continuity too much.

It is not clear that the view Ratzinger holds on this question would have escaped the condemnation issued in 1907 by the office he now heads. It is also ironic that today it is not the papalists but the liberation theologians who — as we shall see — trace the origin of the church (though not its present organizational form) directly back to Jesus and the band of disciples who proclaimed the coming Kingdom in Palestine. The argument goes on but the players appear to have changed sides.

From his present celestial vantage point, it must amuse Alfred Loisy to notice that although he was condemned for suggesting some discontinuity between Jesus and the church, today — eighty years later — it seems that it is putting *too much* emphasis on the continuity that troubles the prefect of the Sacred Congregation and his supporters. This is odd, but true. Their opponents worry that the continuous attempts by liberationists to reach back through the Resurrection to the prophet of Galilee endanger what Hans Urs von Balthasar, one of the Latin Americans' most respected critics, calls the "eschatological" significance of Jesus, his eternal meaning for all times and all places. For the same reason, he is suspicious of biblical scholars, many of them Catholics, who investigate the titles the New Testament applies to Jesus, such as "Son of Man" or "Messiah," trying to find out what they actually meant in the Judaism of the day. He places great weight on the fact the St. Paul, in proclaiming the death and Resurrection of Christ, saw no need to say anything at all about the historical Jesus. He suspects that trying to go back before what he calls the "definitive stratum" of Christian faith, the Resurrection accounts, will inevitably endanger the whole idea of Jesus as the Christ.

If Sobrino states the liberation position even more clearly than Boff does, von Balthasar takes the other side more firmly than Ratzinger. He strongly opposes trying to be something he calls in German a *"Jesuaner'* ("Jesus-ian") both because the actual life of Jesus of Nazareth, he believes, remains hidden in historical shadows, and also because such a person — in view of the impossibility of knowing anything about him with real certainty — can hardly be claimed to have universal "eschatological" significance. Again, one cannot help wondering how these views, now expressed by a strong papalist and one of Ratzinger's most articulate supporters, would have fared under the scrutiny of those who issued *Lamentabili* not all that long ago. But where does that leave today's debate?

Both sides insist that "Jesus" and "Christ" must always be held together. But for Boff and Sobrino, Jesus gives the *content* to Christ, while for Ratzinger and von Balthasar his being *the* Christ is what ultimately is essential about Jesus. The liberation theologians contend that the life and teachings of the Nazarene give substance to the Christ of faith. It was not just anyone who was raised on Easter, it was a particular man, along with what he said and did. Their critics think this emphasis loses the essential combination by putting too much weight on "Jesus." Von Balthasar, who is sometimes called "the pope's favorite theologian," frequently makes this case against going back to Jesus, ending the argument in one book with the stern Latin warning *Aut Christus aut nihil* (either Christ or nothing).[4]

Some people might find this whole debate exotic or even a little precious. But its importance becomes clearer when the practical implications of the two sides are spelled out. In 1977, two years before Ratzinger became prefect, von Balthasar served on the theological commission that met in Rome and issued the first official Vatican criticism of liberation theology. The commission's document, which von Balthasar helped write, voiced a complaint that would be repeated frequently in the following years. It accused the new movement of "politicizing" the church. Later, in an article in the French theological journal *Nouvelle Revue Théologique,* von Balthasar explained why he joined the condemnation. His article is important because it illustrates how his suspicion of putting too much weight on the Jesus of the Gospels leads him to depreciate the Hebrew Scriptures and the role of the faith of Israel should play in the interpretation of the New Testament. In turn, this produces a fundamentally different practical outcome as well.

In this article, von Balthasar's position on the Hebrew Scriptures (which is virtually identical with Ratzinger's) can be stated quite simply: Jesus Christ puts an absolute end to the "old covenant." Israel is replaced by the church. The Jewish way of approaching God is totally *superseded* by the Christian way. The Chosen People are supplanted by the Bride of Christ. The Easter break is absolute. Theologians call this the "supersessionist" the-

ory of the relation of Israel to the church because it holds that
Christianity supersedes Judaism. Most liberation theologians reject it. They hold that Jesus can be understood properly only in
continuity with the faith of Israel and in the light of the Hebrew
Scriptures. Of course both parties confess Jesus as the Christ, but
for the liberationists this confession, far from cutting Jesus off from
his Jewish roots, underlines the importance he himself attached to
his calling as a prophet in the tradition of Amos and Jeremiah.

Not all liberation theologians state this continuity of Christian
and Israelite faith so clearly. Indeed there are passages in Boff's
earlier work (when — ironically — he was relying more heavily on
Ratzinger) where he also leans toward a supersessionist view.[5]
Nonetheless, the tendency in more recent liberation theology is
to emphasize that the ministry of Jesus, instead of superseding
the mode of God's acting in the past, extended and deepened it.
As we shall see, in their practical outcomes, especially in their as-
sessments of the role of the poor in the church, the importance of
these two different starting points is considerable. It could be argued that every political and pastoral issue on which the two sides
disagree stems in one way or another from this primal divergence.
Which side is closer to the truth?

Admittedly the supersessionist position that von Balthasar and
Ratzinger take — that the Christian church has definitively replaced Israel as the new "people of God" — has been the dominant
one for centuries. But starting about two decades ago, spurred by
the painful recognition that the supersessionist view may well have
contributed to the anti-Semitism that culminated in the Holocaust,
scholars began rethinking both the biblical evidence itself and this
inherited theological depreciation of the Jews. The consensus of
this work, including that of Catholic scholars, now tilts very heavily
against the supersessionist view. What has called it into question
are both the accumulating evidence of current biblical scholarship
and the weight of Catholic and Protestant theological interpretation. The continuity between Judaism, Jesus, the Palestinian
"Jesus Movement," and the first decades of the church is becoming increasingly clear with every new archeological find and each
new discovery of an ancient manuscript.

At the theological level, the prefect's position is also more and
more a minority one. Catholic theologians are increasingly turning
to "discipleship" rather than "representing" as the most integral

quality of the church. This is going on in circles quite removed
from liberation theology. Some theologians have recently begun to
advocate a conception of the church that sees its whole history as a
continuous testimony to the significance of Jesus and of attempts to
follow him. Such a conception of the church, as Francis Schüssler
Fiorenza says, "would make discipleship the basic model of the
church." He wisely adds, however, that such discipleship "is not
simply imitation or an immediate following of the historical Jesus."
Rather discipleship today must recognize that the context within
which Jesus lived is different from ours and that therefore our
discipleship requires continuous new interpretations.[6]

So far, however, the more prefectural thinkers, who postulate
a strictly post-Resurrection church, are not persuaded either that
this mounting historical evidence should cause them to alter their
opinions or that the emerging theological emphasis on continuity is
acceptable. The friars and the prefects disagree not on the evidence
itself, but on what it means. Meanwhile their different views of how
much weight to assign the Hebrew Scriptures and the Judaism of
Jesus produce very different ways of reading the same gospel text
and show up in the clashing political ethics of the two sides.

Because he is so widely respected and so influential, and because he expresses his ideas so lucidly, von Balthasar provides the
best example of the position held by the opponents of liberation
theology on the Hebrew Scriptures. He grants that the God of the
ancient Israelite faith did indeed promise liberation to the people
in a language that clearly included the political dimension. In the
Hebrew Scriptures, he agrees, "poor" never meant just "spiritually poor." But for von Balthasar, God spoke such coarse and
earthly language only because in the culture of ancient Israel religion and politics were still mixed. In the New Testament however,
he says, all this is completely changed. Salvation is no longer
merely promised, it is definitively realized; and in the process the
very meaning of the word "salvation" is radically altered. Salvation
or "liberation" (since von Balthasar, like the liberation theologians,
is willing to use the two words interchangeably) no longer has any
historical or lineal aspect at all. It has become transcendental.

This supra-historical point of reference supplies von Balthasar
with his key interpretive principle. And once it is in place, it seems
that there is little that can shake it. For example, Jesus clearly
taught his disciples to pray for the coming of the Reign of God

"on earth," which sometimes creates problems for those who believe that God's Reign is entirely transcendental. Von Balthasar handles this difficulty by giving the prayer a strictly individual meaning. He holds that in this prayer Jesus is placing *himself* at God's disposal as the vehicle of the Heavenly Reign and asking his followers to do the same. He is telling them to give up all efforts to control their own lives in order to be available for this divine reality "unto death" since, as von Balthasar says, "he who is not yet willing to give himself unto death has not yet really given himself." Indeed the ultimate expression of the fact that they are fully God's and no longer their own is that the coming of the Kingdom "lies in a dimension which is beyond life and death."[7] Thus in von Balthasar's translations, "Thy kingdom come on earth" becomes "may the eternal Kingdom come in and through me."

The practical outcome of this interpretation is obvious. It means, for those who follow von Balthasar, the prayer of Jesus for God's Reign to come on earth and for daily bread holds out no hope whatever for bread or deliverance in *this* world. Even in pre-Christian Judaism, von Balthasar says, such utopianism had already been purified from its immanental, this-worldly limitation by merging the prophetic (historical) and the apocalyptic (transcendental) parts of the Jewish tradition. Nonetheless, he insists that still today the hope of Israel remains a mere "dynamic projection into emptiness" unless the Resurrection of Jesus gives its forward looking hope a *real* basis. Christianity is not less utopian than Judaism, he says, but it is *real-utopisch,* realistically "utopian."[8] The contrast does not cast Judaism in a particularly favorable light.

As the prefects read it, the Hebrew Scriptures do *not* help us understand the New Testament. Quite the opposite. We can only know what Amos, Jeremiah, and the Suffering Servant songs really meant in the light of the Apostles. The result of this Christian theology is that some parts of the Hebrew Scriptures are interpreted in a spiritual sense while others are simply abandoned as having been displaced by the New Testament. Christianity has *succeeded* Judaism. Although von Balthasar does not deal with the issue, it is hard to see how, on the basis of his theology, there remains any legitimate religious or theological role for Judaism in the world at all. It would appear to be an anachronism.

One key outcome of God's replacement of Israel by the church, the prefects say, is that religion and politics must no longer be mixed. They insist that, as theologians, they are not only against the *particular* political goals that Boff and his co-workers endorse but that they oppose *any* theologically sanctioned political engagement at all. They believe the liberation Jesus brings to the world is in no sense whatever economic or social, or anything else that smacks of earthly bondage and liberation. It is, says von Balthasar, something infinitely greater, a liberation from the fetters of Satan. This radical difference in interpretive starting points colors everything the liberation theologians and their critics say, about God, Christ, apostolicity, the role of the poor in the church, and the responsibility of the church in the world. Is there any way to resolve this debate?

Francis Schüssler Fiorenza believes that most of the theological work on the nature of "apostolicity" is still to be done. Ratzinger insists that the actual historical circumstances of the death of Jesus, on which the liberation theologians lay such stress, do not really matter.[9] Schüssler Fiorenza argues, however, that Christian theology simply cannot escape raising the question of what it was about Jesus, his proclamation, his actions, that led to his execution. He grants that the faith that emerged after Easter obviously included vital elements that went beyond the pre-Easter experience of Jesus, but as he says, these must be seen *in relation to* who and what Jesus was: "Belief in Jesus as the Christ is ultimately a decision about the significance of the historical Jesus."[10] The emergence of the church is a spelling out, a making explicit, and even a realization of the meaning of Jesus. But how does this happen? These, Schüssler Fiorenza says, are the questions theology must explore in order to show how the church was founded, if not *by* Jesus, then "on" or "in" him. Does the approach of liberation theology have anything to say about how such an exploration might go on? I think it does. But we must delay discussing it until we examine what the contending parties say about the other three essential marks of the church, because they all bear on each other.

19.

Holiness and Praxis

The debate about the mark of the church's holiness comes up with the issues the Boff case raises about *religión popular,* religious populism, dissent, and grassroots movements. At first the connection is not so evident. Perhaps because of our secular atmosphere today, the word "holiness" sometimes evokes overtones of the spectral or the uncanny. Or it suggests some unattainable degree of moral perfection. But the word "holy," as it is used in the Bible, has another force. It means "whole" and is derived from the same root as "heal" and "health." We have a helpful hint to its derivation in the English phrase "hale and hearty." This suggests that God promises the church a certain kind of health that is necessary for its task of healing the hurts of the nations and helping the world itself become whole. Thus at least in some measure the church should *be* what it talks about: whole. But its holiness should *not* call undue attention to itself. Its wholeness or holiness is strictly instrumental. It is intended ultimately not for the church's own benefit but for the world's.

Both the liberationists and their opponents accept the mark of holiness as essential, and both agree that it means God both gives holiness and wholeness to the church and expects them from the church. But from there on disagreements set in. Traditional catholic theology has often viewed the church as a kind of repository holding God's gift of holiness "like a treasure in an earthen vessel." God bestows this holiness on the world *through* the church, by means of its teaching and its sacraments. Furthermore there are always individuals within the church, the saints, who became particularly luminous mediums of God's holiness. Not only are these holy people held up as moral exemplars, they are often believed to have the power to heal. The custom the Catholic church

retains of requiring proofs of healing before a deceased person can
be officially canonized as a saint may seem quaint, but it preserves
the ancient connection between health, holiness, and exemplary
goodness.

For their part, liberation theologians emphasize that "holiness"
refers to the *whole* church and not just to extraordinary persons.
The New Testament (1 Peter 2:9) speaks of the entire people of
God as a "holy nation." This suggests that the whole church, and
not just a few individuals within it or certain of its acts, must in
some way be an *example* of what it is teaching. The problem is
that clearly this is not always the case. It seems easier in practice
for Mother Church to condemn the injustice and corruption of the
sinful world than to admit she often shares this lack of wholeness
in her own life, a failure that makes her message sound like a pot
calling a kettle black. It was for pointing out this embarrassing
contradiction so unsparingly and in such grim detail in his book
Church: Charism and Power that Leonardo Boff got his Alitalia
ticket to Rome. For the liberation theologians, God is helping
the church — as a people — to bring wholeness to the world. It is
holy, but it is not exempt from human failures, or from the equally
human need to repent and be forgiven. Therefore, in order to be
the humble exemplar it is intended to be, the church must not
be afraid to admit its own flaws and ask God's help in correcting
them. In fact, this willingness to concede one's own imperfections
is one expression of exemplary holiness. A "wounded healer" is
often in a better position to heal others, but only when the healer
recognizes her own woundedness.

The special contribution of liberation theology to the discussion about what constitutes the holy or exemplary quality of the
church appears most clearly in its idea of "orthopraxis." Sometimes this word is mistakenly counterposed to "orthodoxy" and
is then said to mean little more than "actions speak louder than
words," or that the church's actual conduct in the world says more
than its preaching. But the idea of orthopraxis is more nuanced
than that. It goes well beyond the familiar idea that faith entails
both belief and action. It suggests that the two are no more than
different moments in the same total response, that they constantly
interact with each other. The idea of "praxis," from which orthopraxis comes, challenges both Descartes and Dewey, both the old
idealistic notion that all actions are derived from previous ideas,

as well as the reductive modern theory that holds that thinking is little more than a reflection of the organism's acting.

Once again Franciscan spirituality provides a good example of orthopraxis. The early Franciscans did not disdain preaching. They proclaimed the message of the gospel in meadows and markets wherever they roamed. But they believed this gospel required them to demonstrate as best they could, in their own lives, what following Jesus meant. St. Bonaventure taught that the same uncreated "inner light" illuminated both thought and action. St. Francis himself believed not only that Christians should *love* the poor but that they came to know Christ *in* the poor. Consequently, these early friars also had a preferential option for the poor. However, they dealt with poverty through a form of compassion in which they sought to know the "poverty of Christ" in the actual poor people of their time. The present-day friars, on the other hand, want to fuse compassionate knowing and doing in a way that might help change the world and contribute to justice rather than merely to charity. They speak therefore of "accompanying" the poor in their struggle against oppression. Still, in their own way, both the early friars and the liberationists, their latter day successors, exemplify the idea of orthopraxis.

Liberation theology thus combines the old and the new. It does not differ from conventional theology principally in the ideas it advances, but in its understanding of what theology is: namely, the effort to help the church become "holy" so that it can be a credible bearer of its message in its own life. But can the actual church exemplify reconciliation in a world so cruelly split up between races and sexes; between Overeaters Anonymous and malnourished children; those with enormous power, who are wary and uneasy, and those with no power, who are restive and resentful? In such a world, the church itself, because it lives within history and not in some transcendent realm, is also inevitably torn and dismembered. Those who share the body of Christ are supposed to be examples. Still Christians rob, kill, cheat, and maim each other with disconcerting regularity. But if God's will for the world is love, reconciliation, and justice, then one of the church's primary tasks is to exemplify these qualities in its own life. This is what holiness means. How, given its own obvious brokenness, can the church nurture and advocate the wholeness of the nations?

Many conventional theologians deal with this dilemma by advocating a transcendental definition of the church's exemplarity. The world may indeed be riven with conflict, they say, but in principle Christ has already reconciled these divisions on the cross. Slumlords and tenants, muggers and victims, revolutionaries and reactionaries may be at each other's throats outside the doors of the sanctuary, but — it is argued — around the altar these differences should be temporarily set aside, while, in the sacrament of Christ, everyone savors the ultimate peace and unity they possess in God. In this view, to involve the church on one side of any of these divisions is terribly dangerous because it could exclude certain people from the single place or occasion that might afford them a taste of wholeness. This is one reason why the critics of liberation theology look with such deep suspicion on what they regard as its advocacy of a partisan church. Individual Christians, they say, can and should engage in such activities. But not the church.

The liberation theologians are not satisfied with this transcendental definition of holiness. They believe too much focus on eternal wholeness can be misused to paper over temporal divisions and lull people into accepting inequities rather than doing something about them. This is why they welcome movements whose purpose is to diminish the ugly rifts between rich and poor, or between dominant elites and cast-off minorities. They will not settle for a church that merely talks about God's justice, or worse, one that declares that in the light of eternity all earthly injustices are insignificant. They want church people to play a role in working for real community in the actual world, even though the community achieved will always remain partial and fragile.

Should the church, as such, and not just individual Christians, become involved in controversial and divisive efforts to achieve human justice? With respect to this question the liberation theologians appear to be closer to Rome's most recent social teaching than their critics admit. In 1971, the Synod of Bishops, which includes bishops from the whole world, meeting in Rome, issued a document entitled *Justice in the World,* which reads in part: "Action on behalf of justice and participation in the transformation of the world appear to us as a constitutive dimension of the preaching of the gospel or, in other words, of the Church's mission for the redemption of the human race and its liberation from every oppressive situation." The key words here are "constitutive" and "the church's mission." The obligation to help transform the world is not viewed as secondary or derivative; and it is not assigned just to individual Christians but to the whole church.

For liberation theology holiness has little to do with spookiness or claims of moral superiority. The holiness of the church means the embeddedness of the entire people of God in a suffering world, in which hope must be concretely exemplified and religious language must point to genuine possibilities of deliverance from the real sins of impoverishment, exclusion, and cynicism. This is why these theologians see a particularly winsome expression of holiness in the Christian base communities.

Base communities are forms of the church in which the promises of God actually become tangible, if only in a provisional manner. They are made up of people from the "base," the lower rungs of society, whose effort to build a more just world and a more inclusive church are not a mere avocation but a life-and-death matter. Since they are the people who have been actually, not just symbolically, deprived and excluded, they are not satisfied with theologies of symbolic or supra-historical reconciliation. They need a holy church so they can be included, and they want the church to help shape civil polities in which they can participate so they will no longer be cast as victims and outsiders. In the course of this search, they discover apostolicity and holiness: apostolicity because the story of Jesus' life informs and inspires their efforts; holiness in the fragile base communities that provide a foretaste of what they are looking for in this world and the next.

Holiness also touches on the question of dissent in the church. Along with many other people today, liberation theologians yearn for a church that is more open and compassionate in its treatment of disagreement. This has always been a difficult issue for the Catholic church, and for other churches as well, in part because of the assumption, which has continued to thrive for centuries within Christianity, that belief is primary and that action stems from a prior idea or conviction. When the church has condemned ideas, it has most often been engaging in a mistaken form of prophylaxis. Its condemnation was intended to prevent the division, schism, sin, or scandal that would presumably stem from taking action on the basis of what authorities viewed as wrong belief.

It is unlikely that the deep-seated differences between the friars and the prefects about the holiness of the church or any other issue will be settled in the near future. In the meantime, what the liberation theologians propose is that perhaps the debate can best be pursued today by transposing the key. They suggest that instead of a war of abstract ideas it become instead a practical discussion about how to make the gospel known and how to *demonstrate* it, so that everyone can see it means more than mere words. A variety of theologies would be welcomed, so long as they all contribute to the increase of compassion and holiness.

A particularly good example of how this transposition to the realm of praxis might expedite theological discourse can be found in the difficult area of Christian dialogue with non-Christian religious traditions. The holy, either as the awe-inspiring or the exemplary, can hardly be restricted to Christianity. Buddhists also seek wholeness, and Hindus nurture holy women and men. How is the church to recognize holiness in a world that is religiously pluralistic?

For many years, theologians sympathetic to liberation theology usually conceded that it had little to teach anyone about religious pluralism. Latin America, after all, is an overwhelmingly Christian continent, at least in its cultural tradition. There are few Buddhists or Hindus or Moslems; so Latin Americans have little experience to draw on to face the world religions. Also, where there are other religious traditions in Latin America (indigenous and African), the liberation theologians have not done much to respond to them. But in more recent years, scholars whose main preoccupation is global religious diversity have begun to appreciate the contribution liberation theology could make to this discussion as well.[1] How might this happen?

Once again, liberation theologians help first by moving the focus from the abstract level to the practical one. As this occurs, it soon becomes clear that religions do not exist apart from their local manifestations. Further, the local expressions of a tradition vary markedly from place to place. Except in the minds of textbook writers there is no such thing as Buddh*ism* or Hindu*ism,* or Christian*ity* for that matter. Studying and comparing the *Bible,* the *Koran,* and the *Sutras* is essential, but it can be misleading unless one understands what these texts actually mean to real people, something that changes from time to time and place to place. Liberation theology helps us understand that genuine inter-religious dialogue only occurs when we recognize how a tradition actually works in people's lives. Those who ignore this insight soon find themselves touring a never-never land of "religions" that do not exist, except possibly in comparative religion monographs.

Liberation theology's down-to-earth approach will help, but it will also make inter-religious conversation, which is already an arduous undertaking, even more difficult. Christians committed to genuine dialogue with other religions can no longer be content to deal merely with the library versions of these faith traditions. Nor can they complain that actual existing expressions of Buddhism or Islam today are corrupted or decadent or "politicized" (as though "pure" editions existed once upon a time). A so-called inter-religious dialogue that directs itself not to actual people but to the platonic ideal of what this or that religious tradition "ought to be" leads nowhere.

Religion, like culture, is a mixed blessing. The truth is that, everywhere religion exists, we can be sure — given the reality of human nature — some people are trying to use the gods to dominate, frighten, or oppress someone else. Indeed any honest attempt at inter-faith dialogue must deal with the ugly fact that our century has not only spawned hundreds of new religious movements but that some of them are destructive and demonic ones. Were the Christians of Japan wrong to try to shun the State Shinto which was used during World War II to lead their nation to ruin? Was Bonhoeffer merely being narrow-minded when he refused to be cozily ecumenical with the "Deutsche Christen" who supported the Nazis? A bland tolerance that sees anything religious as good will simply not do.

Faced with this need to "grade" religious practices, some people just give up. They wearily suggest that maybe we should simply declare a kind of moratorium both on proselytizing and on inter-religious discussion: why do we not just let each other be? If proselytizing is out because it is imperialistic, but neutrality is also not possible because there are obviously positive and negative elements in all religious movements, why not just keep to ourselves — live and let live? The idea is not without its attraction.

But this course is impossible as well. Today, people travel at the speed of sound and ideas at the speed of light. It is futile and mistaken to hope that various cultures and religions could simply leave each other alone. That is no longer possible, if it ever was. As long as people trade and travel and read and watch TV, they will also meet and talk and argue and fall in love and marry each other. There will always be interaction of some kind. The question is not how to avoid the inevitable dialogue, but how to enter into it without losing sight of the equally unavoidable need to make judgments and take sides where necessary.

We have already suggested that, if Christianity had followed more closely the route mapped by St. Bonaventure, the follower of Francis, rather than St. Thomas, the disciple of Aristotle, our current understanding of Christianity and the purpose of the church might be quite different. It is also possible that a more Franciscan form of Christianity might be able to enter more sympathetically into the alternative "way of being" encoded in other faiths. In addition, liberation theology's foundational commitment to the poor provides a key question to ask about our own as well as other faiths: do they bring dignity and hope to the downtrodden? By pressing this query, liberation theology can make a direct contribution to inter-religious dialogue, and thereby to the reconciliation of the whole human family — the ultimate objective of the church.

20

Catholicity and
Cultural Pluralism

Catholicity, another traditional mark of the church, means universality or all-inclusiveness. But how can any church claim to include all when in most areas of the world Christians constitute small minorities and when the world itself is culturally piebald and religiously pluralistic? The answer often given to this question is that catholicity should mean "culturally inclusive." It should signify the church's hospitality to all tongues and nations, its willingness to sink roots in any soil, and its freedom from captivity to any one tribe. What especially annoyed the Brazilian bishops about the Boff silencing was that it seemed to them an expression of European cultural imperialism. It did not allow the church in Brazil to "be Brazilian." It appeared to be a violation of the principle of catholicity. Asian and African Christians often join the Latin Americans in rejecting Rome's insistence that every theology and every liturgy, no matter what its cultural matrix, must eventually be judged by what they view as European or Roman standards, even if these standards are touted as those of the universal church. Cardinal Ratzinger, like most modern churchmen, is in favor of a culturally inclusive church. But, as the *Report* makes clear, he is deeply worried that regional or ethnic particularities could overshadow what he describes as "essentially catholic about Christianity."

How can catholicity and cultural diversity be reconciled? Enrique Dussel, the Argentine theologian, likes to quote the famous dictum of the Indian Cardinal Paracattil, "The Catholic church is neither Latin nor Greek nor Slav, but universal. Unless the church can show herself Indian in India, and Chinese in China, and

Japanese in Japan, she will never reveal her authentically Catholic character."[1] If Dussel is right, and to be universal means to be present within every culture, then a truly "catholic" church would not only allow but encourage a thousand flowers to blossom. It would recognize that different climates nurture different flowers.

But this only states the issue. It does not resolve it. All that blossoms does not necessarily bear fruit. As Ratzinger might put it, eventually one must distinguish flowers from poison ivy, healthy diversity from proliferating malignancy, the genuine from the spurious. The Latin Americans recognize this too. But the question is how?

The principal difference between the prefects and the friars on the question of catholicity is that the former claim it is a quality that *already exists* in the Catholic church. It is indeed the name by which that church is most commonly known. Therefore it is cherished as an invaluable asset, as a gift from God that the church can share with other religious bodies (which can now be called "churches") and eventually with the whole world. To become "catholic," according to this interpretation, is to become a part of the Catholic church and of its beliefs, values, stories, and meaning patterns. Consequently, it means becoming, at least in some way, a participant in "catholic culture," whatever that may mean.

For the liberation theologians, on the other hand, catholicity is indeed a gift, but it is also a task. In our new age of global pluralism it can be realized only when the church is "de-Europeanized," when it is released from its captivity to one culture so that it can enter fully and deeply into others. They believe catholicity is present in the Roman Catholic church today more as a promise than a reality, more as a goal than an accomplished fact. Consequently, it must not only be shared, it must also be sought. At the level of theology this quest for catholicity requires what Eduardo Hoornaert calls "de-northification," the leaving behind of bondage to "northern" (European and American) forms of thought, not so either church or theology can be culture-free, which is both impossible from an anthropological perspective and entirely non-Catholic, but so they can enter in fruitful fusions within other cultures as well.

At the heart of this dispute over catholicity loom the figures of Aristotle and Plato, St. Thomas and Duns Scotus, and the very old question of the proper relationship of the particular to the universal. But in exploring the contrasting understandings of the church's catholic quality one finds in the debate today, it is important to notice how the terms of the discussion have shifted in recent history.

In the late eighteenth and early nineteenth centuries it was the adherents of the Enlightenment who voiced the main attack on Christianity's claim to be universal. Christianity, they said, was not universal enough. It was no more than one particular religion and a rather narrow one at that, which merely made groundless and pretentious claims to be universal. They contended that if there was a universal religion, it was the religion of reason or perhaps a deistic faith in a distant but benevolent Supreme Being. They rejected Christianity, in other words, for being too particularistic. But they still enthusiastically accepted the need for some kind of universal or "catholic" system of spirituality. Some, like Chateaubriand, thought they had discovered this unspoiled original spirituality among the simple savages of the new world, uncorrupted by priestcraft and dogma. In the late twentieth century, however, the argument took a new turn. After the ravages of fascism and the totalitarian threat, critics voiced a different and nearly opposite judgment. Now they accused Christianity of being dangerous because it was *too* universal. It was both a cause and an effect, they said, of the obsessive modern need to unify, control, homogenize, and level out differences. They blamed it for the same desire to inflict monochrome uniformity that others traced to patriarchy or Hellenism or scientism, but which had reached its horrid climax in Hitler's *Gleichschaltung,* the ultimate attempt to erase differences and make everyone the same.

This inverted the terms of the debate. The critics of Christianity's universalism no longer held that it was merely a disguised form of particularism, but that the goal of universality itself was incipiently totalitarian. This reproach is advanced with particular ardor today by French thinkers, especially the disciples of Michel Foucault. They hold that any universal and inclusive system — philosophical, political, or religious — will inevitably become a tyranny that squeezes out minorities and dissenters. They detect a hidden imperialism in all universalizing movements. Christianity should be rejected not because it fails to be universal but because it tries to be and, at least in some measure, succeeds.

It does little good to point out that these two criticisms trap

Christianity in contradictory indictments. The fact is that historically Christianity has been both too narrowly particularistic and also too pretentiously universal, often at the same moment. After the first few decades of its life as a Jewish sect, it became intermeshed first with Hellenistic culture and later with that culture's European heir, both of which saw themselves as incipient universal worlds with a mission to the uncivilized parts of the earth. Soon, it was nearly impossible to separate Christianity from the universal claims of its culture. The Spanish conquerors who pillaged Peru and Mexico referred to their own language interchangeably as either *castellano* or *cristiano*. To "speak Christian" meant to communicate in the language of Christendom. Later, just as a worldwide Christianity became possible in the nineteenth century, the Catholic church froze its language and thought forms into what it held to be the ideal pattern of thirteenth-century Europe, but tried at the same time to make this particular culture the vehicle of a universal religious community. Ugandans were expected to say mass in Latin, and Japanese to ponder the *Summa*. By the twentieth century, some French Catholics, fearful that the church's growth into a global church would undermine the faith, took the bold step of explicitly identifying Christianity with the culture of Europe. "The faith is Europe," Hilaire Belloc once declared, "and Europe is the faith."

In short the proper synthesis of particularity and universalism needed for a true "catholicity" constantly eluded the church's grasp. The liberation theologians believe that such contradictions, combined with the actual birth in our time of a genuine world church, make a radically new approach to the question of what "catholic" means all the more urgent. They begin the search by suggesting that the catholicity of the church is not an existing quality to be extended. Rather, like the static *"est"* in the discarded version of *Lumen Gentium,* this simple identity should now be set aside. Catholicity, rather, should now be seen, like the Reign of God, as both a divine gift and a goal of human striving. Further, not only is the church's catholicity meant to be a sign or sacrament of the wholeness God intends for the entire world; also the church cannot itself be truly catholic while the societies of this world, whose people make up the church, prey on each other and exclude and marginalize whole segments of their populations. Jesus' own entourage, the embryo of the church, somehow brought together

representatives of the rival factions and alienated peoples of his own
day, including women, Zealots, Pharisees and tax-collectors. This
inclusivity was a visible sign of the Reign of God he announced.
But like the prophets before him, Jesus also taught that the Reign
itself would come in its fullness only when the poor were vindi-
cated, the prisoners freed, and all the nations of the earth could
discard their swords and chariots. As the church contributes to the
healing of the world's wounds and divisions, it also contributes to
its own healing. The church's catholicity and the world's genuine
inclusiveness are part of the same mystery. They depend on each
other.

For the prefects, a more universal and united world is also a
goal of the Catholic church. This helps explain their opposition to
the rampant nationalism of the last two centuries and the support
recent popes have given the UN. But when it comes to religious
and cultural disunity, the Catholic church's official formula for universal accord has not changed: the various parties must come to
recognize that the Roman church is the authentic custodian of
catholicity. Catholicity is not just spiritual or invisible. It takes
historical shape. Consequently, though the Vatican never spells
out exactly what form it must take, the achievement of catholicity
requires incorporation into the visible institution that now nurtures
it, and this in turn requires some form of submission to the papal
authority, which guarantees and symbolizes visible unity. There
are no shortcuts.

The liberationists agree and disagree. They also insist that
catholicity must be real, not just ideal. But they emphasize that
if the quest for catholicity in church and world is to be guided by
the spirit of the poor Christ, then there can be no question of a
universality achieved through submission. Submission by someone
also implies domination by someone else. Domination is always a
false form of universality, and, when it is done in the name of a
man who washed his followers' feet, it is a grotesque anomaly. This
is why the friars have always argued that the symbols of monarchy,
such as the papal tiara and episcopal thrones, that Catholics have
traditionally utilized — often with the best intentions — to symbolize an inclusive spiritual dominion, can be dangerously misleading.
John Paul I, the thirty-three-day pope, may have sensed this. He
refused to accept the tiara during his papal inauguration.

For the friars, Christ himself is the exemplar of the mystery of catholicity. He consistently fought against the barriers and taboos that excluded people from the religious and civil communities of his day, but he did so by becoming a servant, not a monarch. There is no doubt that, in the *Pax Romana,* the Roman Empire of Jesus' time had created the most inclusive, i.e., "catholic," political entity the world had ever seen. But Jesus rejected Caesar's solution. His quarrel with the empire, however, was not about the goal of bringing all the world's diverse communities into one imperium. His argument was about what *sort* of imperium it would be, and *how* it would be instituted. He called it the Reign of God, and said that the power to build it did not come "from this world." The finale of Jesus' life, his face-down with Pontius Pilate, provides the denouement of the clash between polar visions of the meaning of "universal," and of how to bring it about: Christ's way or Caesar's.

Cardinal Ratzinger and his supporters recognize the failure of previous definitions of catholicity as well as the liberationists do. They know that the chances of literally initiating all peoples and nations into the existing Catholic church are very remote. Consequently, in recent years, they too have begun to envision a different form of catholicity, one which teaches that the church, even if only as a tiny minority, should be *present* in all cultures. They have also begun to advocate what they call "inculturation." The word suggests the effort to enter other cultures, not by imposing Christianity, but by allowing it to become thoroughly suffused with the culture itself. If, as Cardinal Paracattil says, the church must be Indian in India and Japanese in Japan, then — so the argument goes — it must immerse itself fully in the symbols and stories, the history and perhaps even the traditional religious systems of these lands. It must in-culture-ate itself.

Just as liberation theologians tend to be suspicious of imperial notions of catholicity, they are also skeptical about most attempts at inculturation, because they are aware of the oppressive ways the church has sometimes sought to insert itself into various cultures. Their apprehensiveness arises from the experience of the underclass people they work with and from whom they have learned that culture itself can be despotic. It can be used to exclude and dominate, for example, when a dominant culture imposes its language or legal codes on subordinate minority ones. Some liberation theologians have personally suffered, and seen their people hurt, by repressive measures taken by authoritarian governments in the name of such potent cultural symbols as "homeland" or "Western Christian civilization" or "patriotic duty." They know first hand how powerful elites can skillfully manipulate cultural patterns, folk beliefs, and pious practices of poor people to keep them in poverty and ignorance. They have learned to be suspicious of advocates of inculturation who do not recognize that culture is never neutral. But they also know that no faith, Christianity included, can exist without some cultural vehicle. The key question then becomes: how can Christianity become an integral part of a culture without perpetuating that culture's injustices?

For liberation theology, the history of Jesus' interaction with his culture hints at the answer to this question. Jesus was fully steeped in the traditional religion of his own people. He was not counter-cultural. Nevertheless he did not hesitate to point out how the elites of his day were misusing this heritage. Jesus invoked old cultural and religious traditions such as the Jubilee Year (which decreed a redistribution of land and the cancelling of debts) in the face of economic inequality. He regularly cited the Law and Prophets against his religious critics. He neither embraced nor rejected culture uncritically. Rather he loved it, reshaped it, and then *used* it against its procrustean distortion. He drew on the psalms and the ritual law of his people to expose those who were exploiting religious tradition for their own gain: "It is written, that my house shall be a house of prayer for all people, but you have made it a den of robbers."

For liberation theologians, the concept of "inculturation" is too uncritical and too formal a term. It lacks content. In line with their emphasis on the model Jesus set for the churches, they prefer "incarnation" as the description of how the church should become present within a culture. Incarnation has more contour because it calls to mind the selective way Jesus himself dealt with culture. It was to highlight the church's need to incarnate itself that Boff chose the title *And the Church Became People* for the book that caused the new storm of protest after the silence.

Cultures exist in a constant state of internal conflict between those who control the symbols of power and those who do not. Inevitably some cultural forms and religious patterns become the tools of tyranny while others provide hope and vision to those who fight against it. The Duvalier family clung to power in Haiti for several decades in part by cruelly exploiting such popular spiritual practices as voodoo. Men still subject women to an undercaste in most parts of the world by appealing to traditional definitions of womanhood, many of them sanctioned by religion. Racism is an integral component of many cultures today. But on the other hand the songs and legends and heroes of tyrannized peoples, often borne by their religious beliefs, have inspired dignity among the despised and fired opposition to despots.

Incarnation differs from inculturation because it recognizes this unavoidably conflictual character of culture. If the church models its approach to cultures on the incarnation of Christ it will not seek to diffuse itself equally throughout all strata. Even less will it work principally with the most powerful and privileged sectors. Rather, if the church practices discipleship and *follows* Christ into a culture, it will position itself, as he did, principally (though not exclusively) among the alienated and the rejected. It will incarnate itself among the people, not as their tribune, but as their servant and companion in struggles and defeats. It will partake in the mystery of the presence of Christ among the poor.

The critics of the liberation theologians view this incarnational model of inculturation with enormous misgivings. To them it seems divisive, perhaps "politicizing." At a minimum, it seems to reduce the universality of Christianity to a new particularism. Is there any way to move this discussion forward? The difference between the two sides on this troubling issue of how to reconcile Christianity's universal task with its obvious particularity goes back to their key disagreement about the Jewishness of Jesus and the relationship of the Old and New Testaments. We have already mentioned the Christian theologies, favored by Ratzinger and his supporters, that make the church a "new Israel." The teaching of the Catholic church on this critical point has not yet been fully clarified. In the 1963 Dogmatic Constitution on the Church, the Vatican declared that "Jews still remain most dear to God." In a sermon at a synagogue in Rome in 1986, the pope called God's covenant with Israel "irrevocable." But in another sermon the same year the pope also said that the church, as the new people of God, "assumes and surmounts" the old one. Then in October 1987, Ratzinger caused further confusion when the conservative Italian magazine *Il Sabato* published remarks of his in which he spoke about the "...reality of Jesus Christ in which the faith of Abraham finds fulfillment." Jews understandably found both the pope's and Ratzinger's re-

marks confusing, and, as Rabbi Marc Tannenbaum, director of
international relations for the American Jewish Committee, put
it, as offering "...no place for Judaism and hence no space for
dialogue."[2] Those, like the pope, Ratzinger, and von Balthasar,
who hold to one or another form of this "supersessionist" theology, sometimes suggest that although the Old Testament is particularistic, the coming of Jesus Christ changed all that: with the
crucifixion and Resurrection, this narrow particularism was tran-
scended and left behind. Christianity, it is said, unlike Judaism, is
by definition a universal faith.

Most liberation theologians believe this formulation is wrong
both historically and theologically. First, Judaism is not just particularistic. The Jewish faith teaches that the people of Israel were
given a universal task at the beginning of their history when God
told Abraham that through him "all the nations of the world will
be blessed." The key words here are "through" and "blessed."
The God of the Bible favors *all* peoples by choosing and working
through a *particular* one. And the favor God grants is *blessing* —
which for the ancient Jews meant health and well-being and long
life — not conversion or domination. As Jewish law developed, it
recognized the rights of non-Jews, the "strangers in the land," to
certain God-given rights, like Sabbath rest. The universal side of
Jewish religion is grounded in God's creation of all peoples, in the
covenant with Noah, and in the promise of a messianic era where
all the just shall dwell in peace.

On the theological level, this particularistic-universal pattern
continues with Jesus. His clash with some — not all — of the Jewish
religious authorities of his time arose not because he questioned the
core teaching of his own faith tradition, but because, like the earlier
prophets, he believed that some of those leaders had distorted and
delimited that teaching. Jesus lived and died a Jew, a passionate
participant in a very particular culture. But what does this mean
for the church today? Did the crucifixion and Resurrection change
this?

The evidence says not. Jesus' dead body was removed from the
cross on Friday just before the sundown that marks the start of the
Jewish Sabbath. We have no mention of the Resurrection until the
women who came to anoint the body on Sunday morning. They
would normally have done so on the day immediately following
the death, but, as good Jews, they waited until Sabbath was over.

The question of when and how the Resurrection itself took place remains a mystery, but the Easter texts clearly teach that God did not intrude into the Sabbath even to bring the Easter event to pass. Even God keeps the Sabbath, and if the risen Christ is the same Jesus who was "crucified under Pontius Pilate" (as the classical creeds state), then he remains Jewish. Christianity has a Jewish messiah. The only universalism Christians can claim is inseparably linked to God's promise of blessing to all nations which was given to a particular people and never rescinded.

The sorry result of Christianity's refusal to acknowledge its rootedness in Jewish particularity was a spurious universalism. Christians soon became blithely unaware of the provincialism of the Graeco-Roman world in which they thoroughly "inculturated" themselves, a civilization with lofty confidence in its own universality and catholicity. But the Greek and Roman ideas of universality had little to do with blessing or servanthood. The Greeks believed the mission of Hellas was to civilize the barbarians whether they liked it or not. The Romans imposed their universal unity through law and the legions. Historically Christianity became as "culture-specific" as any other religion, but it acted as though this culture were somehow already universal. It was not. It was one culture among others. What we need now is a catholicity that recognizes and nurtures particularity.

Ironically, as Christianity gropes its way toward becoming — at last — a world faith, and not a Western religion with outposts and enclaves around the globe, Catholic theologians may have a certain advantage over Protestants. True, the Roman party erred in trying to wed Catholic theology eternally to St. Thomas Aquinas and thus to an idealized Western medieval culture. But Protestants, faced with the same dilemma, made an even more disastrous mistake. They tried, earlier in the present century, to create a theology that ostensibly needed no culture at all. Karl Barth grumbled that *Kulturprotestantismus* was Christian theology's greatest foe. He tried to fashion a theology founded on the naked Word of God that allegedly needed no cultural vehicles. Now, however, it has become clear that *every* theology — including Barth's — must express itself in and through some set of cultural patterns. Consequently some Catholic theologians, having grown accustomed to the old inculturated manner of thinking, do not find it as hard as Protestants do to enter into other cultural systems. The problem is they can often become too uncritical of an environing culture. The Protestant suspicion of uncritical "inculturation," on the other hand, therefore preserves an invaluable balancing insight. The gospel must say both yes and no to a culture at the same time: yes to those parts of it that nurture life, and no to those that perpetuate domination and exclusion.

Perhaps the time has come for Christianity to stop trying to deal with world cultures as it tried to deal with Judaism, by — in the pope's ill-chosen words — "assuming" and "surmounting" them. The model of Jesus is one of serving, not one of surmounting or of merely assuming. Incarnation means not just that God became flesh but that God became human, and the human always includes culture. It is important to emphasize, however, that the incarnation took place not in an abstract or universal culture, but in a particular one, the culture of Israel. Further, God chose to come to the subculture of the poor, the landless, the religiously suspect, and Christ contested those elements of the dominant culture he found oppressive to the human spirit.

Future historians may someday describe Mohandas Gandhi as the man who best exemplified what is essential about Christianity in a non-European culture. But Gandhi neither assumed nor surmounted his own Hindu culture. Fully steeped in it, he nonetheless called it into question whenever it damaged the powerless *harijans* he wanted to liberate. He once scolded a well-intentioned Christian missionary who in his effort to inculturate himself had taken to wearing the saffron robes of a Hindu monk. Gandhi told him that he should take off the robes and wear the simple homespun *khadi* instead. Wearing the *khadi* would identify him as someone who had taken the side of the Indian poor, against both the British and against the privileged Hindus who profited from the rule of the British raj.

The prefects are surely right that catholicity cannot be some airy spiritual feeling. It must take visible shape in the real world, and it must be clearly linked to the apostolic character of the church. But the friars are also correct that catholicity today will require a form of inculturation that takes the self-humbling of God in the incarnation and in Jesus' preference for the underclass as its model; this will require making painful choices and taking sides. It appears certain that the church's catholicity will never be perfected this side of the Reign of God. It also appears that unless Rome is prepared to silence many hundreds of Leonardo Boffs, not just in Brazil but in Taiwan and Ghana and Sri Lanka, the debate about what catholicity is and how it should be pursued can hardly be expected to subside for a long time to come.

21

Oneness and Diversity

The riddle of the one and the many antedates the birth of Christianity by many centuries. But, since the church's earliest years, it has been a major preoccupation of theologians as well. The world is so obviously many. It is peopled by many tongues and nations, many classes and conditions, many philosophies and faiths. Yet Christians confess that God is one and that the church is, or should be, one. But this is exactly what troubles the conscientious critics of liberation theology most: they are genuinely fearful that it threatens the church's unity. They are afraid its partisan stance could tear the flesh of the body of Christ.

It would be idle to belittle their apprehensiveness as totally unfounded. To many observers, the rift that has appeared during the Boff case reveals all the elements of a major schism, such as the ones that devastated the visible unity of the church when Constantinople separated from Rome in 1054, or when the Protestant Reformation erupted in the sixteenth century. Once again today — as then — geography, theology, politics, and personality clashes all seem to be conspiring to drive a divisive wedge into the visible body of the church.

But there are also significant differences between today's situation and the previous schisms. Unlike the earlier instances, both sides in this present conflict accept — at least in principle — the role of the bishops and the pope in maintaining the church's unity. The patriarch of the Orthodox church once excommunicated the bishop of Rome. Martin Luther publicly burned the papal bull that excommunicated him. But nothing of the kind is going on today. When the Pope John Paul II's prefect silenced Leonardo Boff, the friar accepted the silencing and said he preferred to "walk with his church." When Gutiérrez and Sobrino and Boff defend their

178

theologies today, they do so by insisting their ideas are "ecclesial," that they have worked them out in cooperation with the bishops and in service to them. The liberation theologians sometimes differ with the pope, but they accept the principle of papal authority. There seems to be little likelihood that the kind of division that rent the church on those previous occasions will occur again.

But will the visible unity that the church manages to maintain through all the tumult of dissent and diversity, political division and liturgical innovation, be anything more than a façade? If Christian base communities led by lay people, including unordained women, continue to multiply at their current rate, how will bishops actually exercise any real authority over them? If the Vatican is reluctant to excommunicate anyone today, but its public warnings and disciplining of theologians succeed only in getting their ideas a wider hearing, what does that mean for the church's unity? If, as Ratzinger claims, the problem is that old-fashioned styles of heresy have been replaced by heterodox forms of inculturation that strenuously claim to be orthodox, where will it all lead?

The worst possible scenario says that the Catholic church is headed for even more retrenchment and repression, that we have seen only the beginning of a massive attempt at controlling dissent and consolidating hierarchical control, that the worst is yet to come. According to this grim script, lifting the silencing of Leonardo Boff was merely a temporary respite that will be followed by increasingly draconian measures. Unfortunately, the continued attacks on Boff and the warnings of more punishments to come lend some plausibility to this worst-case scenario. But need it be so?

It might be helpful to sketch out a few ground rules that could help facilitate a genuine rather than a spurious unity while at the same time encouraging the necessary debate to follow its course.

1. First, all parties should recognize that the argument has gone on for a long time, in one form or another, since before they were born, so it is unlikely it will be settled in the foreseeable future. This recognition almost automatically carries with it the implication that a certain amount of forbearance and patience will be required. It also suggests that various forms of censorship and silencing are inappropriate and should be avoided. The history of Christianity is too replete with the stories of the various Joans of

Arc, who were burned in one century, only to be canonized in a later one. The French theologians censored by Pius XII became the heroes of the Council fifteen years later. The theological faculty of the University of Paris once burned the books of Thomas Aquinas, and, as we have noted, Cardinal Ratzinger's view that the church is a post-Resurrection phenomenon might well have been condemned by a previous prefect of his own congregation in Rome eighty-five years ago.

Stifling honest debate is morally wrong and counterproductive. If depriving dissidents of their right to speak and publish is evil in the U.S.S.R., it is also wrong in the church. Nor does an involuntary silencing become more acceptable when it is described by those who impose it as an expression of spiritual discipline for the good of the person silenced, as it was in Leonardo Boff's case. Liberation theologians are not averse to silence. Gustavo Gutiérrez has written that one's first response to the presence of God should always be awe, silence, and contemplation. The second should be loving action toward one's neighbor. At best theology comes in third. There can be little doubt that theologians should sometimes choose to be silent, but prefects should not make that decision for them.

2. On the other hand, theologians who decide to explore new avenues of thought and redefinitions of doctrine should not, at the same time, expect to receive the unqualified sanction and endorsement of the hierarchy for everything they write. Father Charles Curran, the American Catholic moral theologian who has run into serious trouble with Rome for taking issue with what he thinks is a mistaken or ill-conceived teaching by the pope or the bishops, has set a good example. He carefully distinguishes in his writing what is the teaching of the church — as interpreted by the pope — and what he thinks it should be. Of course, he also tries to argue for his own view, but when he does so, though he insists his freedom be respected, he does not expect to be recognized by church authorities to be an official interpreter of the standing teaching.

It is obvious to everyone, including the prefect of the Congregation for the Doctrine of the Faith, that the teaching authorities of the Catholic church have been mistaken more than once in the past, and that they have eventually conceded their mistake, sometimes in response to the criticism of theologians and others who openly differed with them. Thus, Father Curran does not pretend that his ideas about artificial contraception, for example, are completely in line with the most recent authoritative statement on this issue in *Humanae Vitae,* so he carefully distinguishes his own position from the encyclical's when he presents it. This is only fair. But it also suggests that his competence as a teacher should not be judged on the basis of whether he *holds* a particular view but on whether he presents it fairly and accurately. This is hardly asking for too much.

3. The more difficult case comes, as Cardinal Ratzinger points out, when theologians claim they, and not the pope or the prefect, are presenting the *true* teaching of the church. Some of this problem could be avoided if all parties in the argument gave up the claim to be stating some final, unamendable interpretation and admitted that all theology, whether of friars or of prefects or of anyone else, is a matter of approximation, of trying to define a reality that ultimately eludes final definition. Still, even if this degree of modesty is reached, what is needed in a dispute is a careful and *bona fide* attempt by all parties concerned to decide at least what the nature of the disagreement is, and not a silencing. In such a dispute, it is always important, especially for the prefects, to maintain with great care the canons of due process and fair procedure. When all else fails, there is nothing wrong with a prefect publicly announcing that a given theologian's teachings are not in conformity with Rome. But this should always be done with respect and dignity. As Boff points out, if higher authorities treat dissenters in the church callously or shabbily, it makes the church's efforts to combat such demeaning practices in the secular world look silly and hypocritical. But this is not the most important reason to respect human rights within the church, for even if their denial had no negative impact on the outside world, violations would be an intrinsic breach of Christian ethics.

4. Perhaps the friars of this age could improve the situation by recognizing that the church will probably always need some prefects. Even St. Francis himself sought the endorsement of the pope (and got it). Leonardo Boff seems to agree with this proposition when he writes, in *Church: Charism and Power,* that there is a charism of leadership, and that the church needs both spirit and structure. Other liberation theologians accept this idea as well, though some more willingly than others. The friars need to give up the fantasy they sometimes indulge in of a church without prefects.

Such a thing will never happen this side of the Reign of Heaven. Even religious institutions, being human, need governance. The question is not how to get rid of prefects but how to keep them honest. Maybe the friars will be able to recognize this more easily when they admit that they themselves have more power *vis-à-vis* the prefects than they admit. At some level the prefects, including the cardinal-prefect of the Congregation for the Doctrine of the Faith, already know this. On their best days they realize full well that dissent and discussion are signs not of sclerosis but of vitality. They know they need the Leonardo Boffs and base communities, or they would eventually have nothing over which to preside as prefects. Religion always requires both spirit and structure. When the friars also recognize how much the prefects need them, they may be able to allow them to exercise the leadership charism Boff says they have, but also to keep them humble while they do it.

5. As for Cardinal Ratzinger and his supporters, the day is not far off when they will have to concede that the basic biblical and theological premises of liberation theology are correct. The church's mission must trace itself back to Jesus himself, or his Resurrection means nothing. The prefectural theologians who still make the hours between the crucifixion and Easter Sunday an impassable gap instead of an unbreakable link between Israel and the church are fighting an uphill battle against a growing mass of theological consensus and biblical scholarship. They have taken the wrong path, and they cannot go on much longer denying the accumulating historical evidence, carefully pieced together by many Catholic as well as Protestant scholars. This evidence says that between the Palestinian rabbi, the Risen Christ, and the early church there is far more continuity than hiatus. Nor can they continue to deny that historical evidence has any theological bearing on our understanding of Jesus and the early church, for to do so is to veer perilously close to what was once called Docetism, the heresy that denied the earthly flesh-and-blood reality of Christ's incarnation. Once the prefects make this admission, then the whole debate about liberation theology, which is now stalled because its critics do not consider the "historical Jesus" a relevant datum, will enter a new phase. This does not mean the Latin Americans and their allies will then win all the arguments, but that a serious debate about who Jesus really was and what he means for us today can begin at last.

If both sides in the current dispute could agree to something like these ground rules, then I believe the much-needed argument could proceed. But the question would still remain: how should the participants conduct the argument?

This is where, in my view, the whole theological world has the most to learn from the liberation theologians. They have developed an enormously promising method: "theology as reflection on praxis." This means they do not do their work in the serene atmosphere of arguments with other theologians alone but in the bruising back-and-forth between acting in the world and careful reflection on that action. This is why liberation theologians are so insistent that their critics do more than read what they have written — which is like overhearing one side of a telephone call — but that they become aware of the actual situation in which they live and work, what they often call the "social reality." In their usage, the "social reality" means what actual people think and do to shape their political and cultural worlds. It also includes the religious ideas and values that shape the way people see and act. For the Latin Americans, theology has a double link with this "reality." First, it *arises* out of reality, pondering and analyzing it in the light of faith. But it has a second link too. It also *guides* the attempt to shape it. Then the cycle begins again. Action shapes thought and thought informs action. Theology becomes not just a dispute about ideas but a resource for real people on how to see themselves and their world, therefore also on what to do. Theology guides action. Action refocuses theology. This continuous process of acting, reflecting, then acting again — all in the light of faith — *is* "liberation theology."

Once one understands this *modus operandi,* the liberation theologians' claim that their method is not particular to Latin America becomes more believable, and so does their strong belief in the positive function of dissent. Dissent is not deviation but an integral part of the process. This also explains why liberation theologians sometimes find holding prolonged discussions with their theological critics over the marks of the church (or anything else) so frustrating. The arguments race past each other, because most conventional theologians, including those who teach at seminaries and those who staff the Sacred Congregation for the Doctrine of the Faith, proceed something like *theoretical* physicists. They work with full confidence that, given sufficient time, differences can be resolved at the level of conceptual exchange. Cardinal Ratzinger himself is a particularly good example of this ideational approach to religious and theological dissensus. Or, he also believes, when all else fails, one must resort to various modes of discipline. On the other hand, liberation theologians work in the manner of *experimental* physicists. If there is a difference of opinion, they are inclined to invite a colleague into the laboratory to observe what happens when the procedure is tried out. Here the laboratory is the Christian community itself as it lives in "the social reality," and the procedure is "praxis," the continuous sequence of action and reflection.

In recent years, liberation theologians have suffered unnecessarily. They have had to endure not only the warnings and silencings meted out by short-sighted prefects but also stinging reprimands even from their friends. They have been scolded because — it is said — they are divisive and not sufficiently committed to dialogue, and they should be in closer communication with the worldwide church and the international theological guild. Maybe one positive outcome of the Boff case is that it makes clear why the Latin Americans feel so misrepresented by this critique. They do not oppose dialogue. They welcome it. They are strong advocates of a truly global church and an authentically catholic Christianity. But they insist it must be made up of distinct communities, critically conscious of their own particularity and speaking to each other with that awareness. They are suspicious of the claims of European or Roman theology to be *the* one universal, catholic theology to which all others must adapt. They have never denied the church's apostolicity. They believe that the people they serve are living apostolically, and the number of Latin American Christians who have suffered martyr's deaths, as the first apostles did, provides some substantiation to their claim.

What kind of "oneness" in the church might the approach liberationists represent eventually lead to? Probably never again to the attempt to devise a single, all-encompassing theological formula — however minimal — to which everyone everywhere must subscribe. Rather, it could lead to the culturally and theologically pluralistic church Karl Rahner once foresaw, united not from the past or from the top, but by its hope for that which is yet to be. The Latin Americans believe they have grounds for hope, since signs and portents of just such a church are already appearing on their own continent. It is a church, which though weak and vulnerable by worldly standards, is nonetheless moving toward apostolicity, catholicity, holiness, and unity. It finds the oneness in its stumbling attempt to follow the poor Christ into the depths of diverse cultures in order to demonstrate the beloved community only God makes possible.

It seems that Karl Rahner, too, toward the end of his life, imagined a church bound together more by this venturesome love than by dictums and dogmas. Maybe that is why one of his last acts was to send a warm letter of support for Gustavo Gutiérrez, who was then under attack by Rome. In any case, writing in his *Theological Investigations*, Rahner said in 1974 that he hoped one day, there will "no longer be any one single and universal basic formula of the Christian faith applicable to the whole church." If that day comes, and welcomed by both the prefects and the friars, by the pope and the Congregation for the Doctrine of the Faith, then the Catholic church will have taken a decisive step toward an authenticity that now seems so elusive. And if it does, all the nations the world — and all the other churches — will be greatly blessed.

The trial of Leonardo Boff is not yet over, nor is the trial of liberation theology. When will we learn that within the church we have had quite enough trials? What is beginning now is the trial of the church itself. That trial will test whether the church can in fact "become the people," and whether Christianity, for so many centuries a largely Western and "northern" faith, can live in and speak to the tribes and nations of the whole world. This will require a good deal of venturesome theology. Obviously, some of that theology will be true and faithful and some will not. What we will need, therefore, is not indictments and censures but patience, humility, and a genuinely open debate. But a debate does not have accusers and defendants. It has partners and protagonists who respect and listen to each other. In a debate no one tries to silence anyone else. Both sides expect to learn from the clash and resolution of ideas. Boff and his fellow liberation theologians know as well as anyone that they are not always right, nor their opponents always wrong. What they ask is not for agreement, but for the opportunity to contribute to the conversation, to speak and to listen.

22

Silencing and Community

Indeed, as the conversation continues, it will no doubt become clear that liberation theology, like every other theology, has no final answers. Human life and history being what they are, the time will come when new voices with concerns we cannot now foresee and perspectives we can scarcely imagine will arise in the household of faith and seek to be heard. But whether the church as a whole will hear and respond to such voices tomorrow depends in considerable measure on whether it learns to heed the cries of the voiceless today. This is why someone's right to be heard within the Christian community is not just a procedural question or a matter of fair play. It has to do with the very nature of the religious community itself.

Leonardo Boff is not the only Christian to be silenced. There have been many before him. And it may be well to remember that the first silencing to occur in the church, and in some ways the primal one, was that of women. The "original silencing" made an impact in some ways analogous to that of original sin: it has stained everything since. Why and how did it happen? It is incontestable that women played critical leadership roles in the early Christian church. Priscilla, for example, seems to have been at least the equal of her husband Aquila in the work they did together as teachers (Acts 18:2, 18, 26; 1 Cor. 16:9; Rom. 16:3). The Apostle Paul taught that women could lead worship and that the sexes were equal before God. In some ways the early Christian movement appears to have been a bold experiment in egalitarian inclusiveness. But as the church began to adjust itself to its environing culture, something changed. In the generation that followed Paul, the male leaders surrendered to the pressure they felt to deprive women of the role they had once played (1 Tim. 2:11–

12). Most scholars now explain the notorious passage in Paul's 1 Corinthians (14:33–35) in which women are admonished to remain silent in the churches — a blatant contradiction of what he says elsewhere — as an insertion that was placed there during the less venturesome generation that followed him.

Whether this was the case or not, the result of this "original silencing," which antedated Leonardo Boff's by nineteen hundred years, was not just to deprive half of the church's members of their full humanity, a wounding that would be serious enough in its own right. It also set an ugly precedent, and it fundamentally distorted the entire structure of Christian worship and teaching. Insofar as it was actually enforced it deprived the community's prayer and hymnody of the symbols that could be brought to it only from the lives of women. It impoverished its ethical life and its diaconal service by assigning less weight to those particular forms of pain that women, as the bearers of children and the objects of patriarchal power, bring to expression. It thinned out the celebration, not just for women, but for everyone, by preventing the unique joys and ecstasies women feel from being shared by all.

The deformation that resulted from the silencing of women is that the whole body was crippled and its capacity to hear anything or anybody seriously attenuated. One cannot tune out some without at the same time tuning out others. By muting the sisters, the early church inflicted on itself a form of deafness that has persisted ever since. Women were the first to be silenced, and in many respects that archetypal silencing continues today. But women were not alone. Once silencing found its way into the company of the faithful, there were others whose songs and stories were also stifled. Women share this disallowance of speech, of saying one's word, with many, many others. Their enforced quiet is also the lot of millions of the world's poor, and of those who are rejected or excluded for a variety of other reasons from full participation in the human family. This is probably why women everywhere have responded with enthusiasm to those theologies that take as their starting point the perspective of the voiceless, a preferential option for the silenced.

In the biblical tradition, God is known as the Holy One who speaks to human beings and who expects them to answer. Therefore, to silence someone, it could be said, is a type of blasphemy. It denies that person the opportunity to respond to God's call, and it therefore denies God. To silence is to fashion a kind of idol, a false God who calls everyone but who does not expect everyone to answer, or who expects some to answer for others. The Christian church, however, understands itself to be a community that is constituted by the Word which God spoke to it in the life of Jesus and to which a response *must* be given. This is why the practice of silencing and excluding stands in opposition to the spirit that is needed if the church is to become an inclusive world church.

Bishop Casaldáliga said it with elegance when, in the poem he wrote at the time of the silencing, he reminded Leonardo that by becoming silent for awhile, he would partake of the condition in which those who have no voice — either in the church or in the world — live all the time. But the hope to which the church gives voice — or should — is that this unnatural silence will not last forever, that by God's grace the mouths of the mute will be unstopped and one day all will sing the Lord's song together.

Notes

2 — The Larger Sagas

1. Karl Rahner, "Towards a Fundamental Theological Interpretation of Vatican II," *Theological Studies*, vol. 40, no. 4, December 1979, pp. 717–718.

3 — The Summons

1. Quoted in Leonardo Boff, "Minha convocação a S.C. para a Doutrina da Fe: um testemunho pessoal," *Grande Sinal*, no. 10, December 1984, p. 779, my translation.

4 — David and Goliath

1. "Outra vez na mira," *Veja*, June 17, 1987, pp. 60ff.
2. *Random House Dictionary of the English Language.*
3. Leonardo Boff, *Passion of Christ — Passion of the World* (Maryknoll, N.Y.: Orbis, 1987).
4. Leonardo Boff, *The Maternal Face of God* (San Francisco: Harper & Row, 1987).
5. Pedro Casaldáliga, "Benedición de São Francisco para Frey Leonardo Boff," *Tempo e Presença*, June 1985, p. 7, my translation.

5 — Francis and Bonaventure

1. Leonardo Boff, *St. Francis: A Model for Human Liberation* (New York: Crossroad, 1982).
2. Cited by José Duque, *La tradición protestante en la teología latinoamericana* (San José, Costa Rica: Departamento Ecuménico de Investigaciones, 1983), p. 63.
3. See Michael Novak, *Will It Liberate? Questions About Liberation Theology* (Mahwah, N.J.: Paulist, 1987).

6 — Charism and Power

1. Leonardo Boff, *Church: Charism and Power: Liberation Theology and the Institutional Church* (New York: Crossroad, 1986), p. 159.
2. Ibid., p. 160.

3. Ibid., p. 161.
4. Ibid., p. 51.
5. Ibid., p. 59
6. Ibid., p. 43.
7. Ibid., p. 38.
8. Ibid., p. 60.
9. Ibid., p. 58.
10. Ibid.
11. Ibid., p. 59.

7 — Brazilians in Rome

1. Sacred Congregation for the Doctrine of Faith, *Instruction on Certain Aspects of the "Theology of Liberation,"* III, 4.

8 — The Brazilian Church and Roman Intervention

1. Pedro Ribeiro de Oliveria, "The Romanization of Catholicism and Agrarian Capitalism in Brazil," *Social Compass,* vol. 26, nos. 2–3, 1979, p. 314.
2. Ibid., pp. 309–329.

9 — The Prefect's Citadel

1. Eamon Duffy, "Urbi, but not Orbi . . . the Cardinal, the Church and the World," *New Blackfriars,* vol. 66, June 1985, p. 272.
2. E. J. Dionne, Jr., "The Pope's Guardian of Orthodoxy," *New York Times Magazine,* November 24, 1985, p. 40.

10 — The Ratzinger Report

1. Joseph Ratzinger (with Vittorio Messori), *The Ratzinger Report: An Exclusive Interview on the State of the Church* (San Francisco: Ignatius, 1986), p. 14.
2. Ibid., pp. 29–30.
3. Joseph Ratzinger, *Rapporto sulla Fede* (Milan: Paolini, 1985).
4. *The Ratzinger Report,* p. 25.
5. Peter Steinfels, review of *The Ratzinger Report,* in *America,* November 30, 1985, p. 388.
6. Quoted in *The Ratzinger Report,* p. 29.
7. Ibid., p. 30.
8. Ibid., p. 45.

11 — Guardian of Orthodoxy

1. *The Ratzinger Report,* p. 176.
2. Ibid.

3. Ibid., p. 177.

4. Peter Hebblethwaite, *John XXIII: Pope of the Council* (London: Chapman, 1984), p. 398.

5. Ibid.

6. Cited by Nicholas Lash, "Catholic Theology and the Crisis of Classicism," *New Blackfriars*, vol. 66, June 1985, p. 283.

7. Duffy, "Urbi, but not Orbi...," p. 278.

8. *The Ratzinger Report*, p. 194.

9. Ibid., p. 166.

10. Lash, "Catholic Theology," p. 28.

12 — The Colloquy

1. Leonardo Boff, "Minha Convocação a Sagrada Congregação para a Doutrina da Fe: um testemunho pessoal," *Revista Eclesiástica Brasileira*, vol. 44, fasc. 176, December 1984, p. 849, my translation.

2. Ibid., p. 850.

3. For the Notification, see *L'Osservatore Romano*, English edition, April 9, 1985. The official Latin version can be found in *Acta Apostolicae Sedis*, vol. 77, no. 8, pp. 758–759.

4. Leonardo Boff, "Minha Convocação," *Revista Eclesiástica Brasileira*, p. 850.

13 — The Silence

1. The words are quoted here from pp. 10–11 of a mimeographed English translation by James and Margaret Goff: "We Have a Lot to Learn from the Nicaraguan Church."

2. Quoted in a mimeographed document of episcopal responses to the Instruction in the diocesan library at Nova Iguaçu, Brazil.

3. "Theologen gegen marxistische Analyse," *Frankfurter Allgemeine Zeitung*, August 2, 1985.

14 — The Easter Gift

1. E. J. Dionne, "Pope Using Theme of Liberationists to Blunt Their Movement," *International Herald Tribune*, April 5–6, 1986.

2. Robert Moynihan, "New Vatican document to stress a preferential love for poor, but will also urge Reconciliation," *National Catholic Register*, March 23, 1986.

3. See *International Herald Tribune*, April 7, 1986.

15 — Romans and Brazilians

1. Kenneth Woodward et al., "Church in Crisis," *Newsweek*, December, 1985, p. 75.

16 — Two Forerunners

1. Thomas F. O'Meara, *Romantic Idealism and Roman Catholicism: Schelling and the Theologians* (Notre Dame: University of Notre Dame Press, 1982), p. 106.
2. Quoted in ibid., p. 149.
3. Ibid.
4. Yves M.-J. Congar, O.P., *A History of Theology*, trans. Hunter Guthrie, S.J. (New York: Doubleday, 1968), p. 183.
5. T. M. Schoof, *A Survey of Catholic Theology 1800–1970* (Glen Rock, N.J.: Paulist Newman Press, 1970), p. 38.

17 — The Marks of the Church

1. Leonardo Boff, *Trinity and Society* (Maryknoll, N.Y.: Orbis Books, 1988).
2. "Arquidiocese do Rio examina novo livro de Boff, affirma d. Eugenio," *Folha de São Paulo*, February 17, 1987, my translation.
3. Ibid.
4. Quoted in "Outra vez na mira," *Veja*, June 17, 1987, p. 62, my translation.

18 — Apostolicity and the Poor

1. John A. Hardon, *The Modern Catholic Dictionary* (Garden City, N.Y.: Doubleday, 1980), p. 35.
2. Joseph Ratzinger, *Theologische Prinzipienlehre Bausteine zur Fundamentaltheologie* (Munich: Erich Wewel, 1982), pp. 456–466; cf. Ratzinger, *Das Neue Volk Gottes: Entwürfe zur Ekklesiologie* (Dusseldorf: Patmos, 1972), pp. 75–89.
3. Jon Sobrino, *The True Church and the Poor* (Maryknoll, N.Y.: Orbis, 1986), p. 183.
4. Hans Urs von Balthasar, *Kennt uns Jesus, Kennen Wir Ihn?* (Freiburg im Breisgau: Herder, 1980), p. 41.
5. Leonardo Boff, *Ecclesiogenesis: The Base Communities Reinvent the Church* (Maryknoll, N.Y.: Orbis, 1986), pp. 45–60.
6. Francis Schüssler Fiorenza, *Foundational Theology: Jesus and the Church* (New York: Crossroad, 1984), p. 172.
7. von Balthasar, *Kennt uns Jesus*, p. 39.
8. von Balthasar, *Elucidations* (London: SPCK, 1975) (first published in German: *Klarstellungen: zur Prüfung der Geister*, 1971), p. 50.
9. Joseph Ratzinger, *Seek That Which is Above* (San Francisco: Ignatius, 1986), p. 51.
10. Francis Schüssler Fiorenza, *Foundational Theology*, p. 107.

19 — Holiness and Praxis

1. Paul Knitter, *No Other Name? A Critical Survey of Christian Attitudes Toward the World Religions* (Maryknoll, N.Y.: Orbis, 1985).

20 — Catholicity and Cultural Pluralism

1. Enrique Dussel, "Theologies of the 'Periphery' and the 'Centre': Encounter or Confrontation," in Claude Geffré, Gustavo Gutiérrez, and Virgil Elizondo, eds., *Different Theologies, Common Responsibility: Babel or Pentecost?* Concilium 171 (Edinburgh: T. & T. Clark, 1984), pp. 87ff.

2. Ari Goldman, "Cardinal's Remarks on Jews Questioned," *New York Times,* November 18, 1987.

Bibliography

By Leonardo Boff

Boff, Leonardo. *O caminhar da Igreja com os oprimidos*. Rio de Janeiro: CODECRI, 1981.

——. *Church: Charism and Power: Liberation Theology and the Institutional Church*. New York: Crossroad, 1986.

——. *O destino do homen e do mundo*. Petrópolis: Vozes, 1973.

——. *E a Igreja se fez povo*. Petrópolis: Vozes, 1986.

——. *Ecclesiogenesis: The Base Communities Reinvent the Church* Maryknoll, N.Y.: Orbis, 1986.

——. *A fe na periferia do mundo*. Petrópolis: Vozes, 1979.

——. *O Franciscanismo no mundo de hoje*. Petrópolis: Vozes, 1981.

——. "A Igreja e a paixão do povo." *Religião e Sociedade,* vol. 1, 1977, pp. 115–118.

——. *Jesus Christ Liberator: A Critical Christology for Our Time*. Maryknoll, N.Y.: Orbis, 1978.

——. *Liberation Theology: From Dialogue to Confrontation*. San Francisco: Harper & Row, 1986.

——. *The Maternal Face of God*. San Francisco: Harper & Row, 1987.

——. "Minha convocação a S.C. para a Doutrina da Fe: um testemunho pessoal." *Grande Sinal,* no. 10, December 1984, pp. 778–790.

——. "Minha convocação a Sagrada Congregação para a Doutrina da Fe: um testemunho pessoal." *Revista Eclesiástica Brasileira,* vol. 44, fasc. 176, December 1984, pp. 845ff.

——. *Passion of Christ — Passion of the World*. Maryknoll, N.Y.: Orbis, 1987.

——. *St. Francis: A Model for Human Liberation*. New York: Crossroad, 1982.

——. *Trinity and Society*. Maryknoll, N.Y.: Orbis Books, 1988.

——. "Una visión no liberadora de la 'teología de la liberación.'" *El País,* January 28, 1985, p. 9.

——. "We Have a Lot to Learn from the Nicaraguan Church." Mimeo copy of English translation from *El Tayacán* (Managua), no. 163, October 12–18, 1985, pp. 10–11. Translation from James and Margaret Goff, Apdo. 3205, Managua, Nicaragua.

Boff, Leonardo, and Clodovis Boff. *Salvation and Liberation*. Trans. Robert R. Barr. Maryknoll, N.Y.: Orbis, 1979.

Boff, Leonardo, and Virgil Elizondo, eds. *The People of God Amidst the Poor*. Concilium 176. Edinburgh: T. & T. Clark, 1984.

By Clodovis Boff

Boff, Clodovis. *Agente pastoral a povo*. Teologia Orgânica 1. Petrópolis: Vozes, 1980.

―――. "A influência política das Comunidades Eclesiais de Base (CEBs)." *Religião e Sociedade*, vol. 4, 1979, pp. 95–119.

―――. *Theology and Praxis*. Maryknoll, N.Y.: Orbis Books, 1986.

Boff, Clodovis (with Leonardo Boff). *Introducing Liberation Theology*. Maryknoll, N.Y.: Orbis Books, 1987.

By Joseph Ratzinger

Ratzinger, Joseph. *Das Fest des Glaubens Versuche zur Theologie des Gottesdienstes*. Einsiedeln: Johannes, 1981.

―――. "Freedom and Liberation: The Anthropological Vision of the Instruction 'Libertatis Conscientia.'" *Communio*, Spring 1987, p. 55.

―――. *Introduction to Christianity*. Trans. J. R. Foster. New York: Seabury, 1979.

―――. *Kardinal Ratzinger der Erzbischof von München und Friesing in Wort u. Bild mit dem Beitrag "Aus Meinem Leben."* Munich: J. Pfeiffer, 1977.

―――. "München und Rom: Epochen und Pole der Katholizität" (lecture given on the occasion of his elevation to cardinal, July 10, 1977). Munich: Eos, 1977.

―――. *Das Neue Volk Gottes: Entwürfe zur Ekklesiologie*. Dusseldorf: Patmos, 1972.

―――. *Rapporto sulla Fede*. Milan: Paolini, 1985.

―――. *Schauen auf den Durchbohrten Versuch zu einer spirituellen Christologie*. Einsiedeln: Johannes, 1984.

―――. *Seek That Which is Above*. San Francisco: Ignatius, 1986.

―――. *Theologische Prinzipienlehre Bausteine zur Fundamentaltheologie*. Munich: Erich Wewel, 1982.

――― (with Vittorio Messori). *The Ratzinger Report: An Exclusive Interview on the State of the Church*. San Francisco: Ignatius, 1986.

――― (with Hans Urs von Balthasar). *Maria, Kirche im Ursprung*. Freiburg: Herder, 1980.

Books in English

Balthasar, Hans Urs von. *Elucidations.* London: SPCK, 1975. (First published in German: *Klarstellungen: zur Prufung der Geister,* 1971.)

Barreiro, Alvaro. *Basic Ecclesial Communities: The Evangelization of the Poor.* Maryknoll, N.Y.: Orbis, 1982.

Berryman, Phillip. *The Religious Roots of Rebellion.* Maryknoll, N.Y.: Orbis, 1984.

Bramel, Ernest, and C.F.D. Moule. *Jesus and the Politics of His Day.* Cambridge: Cambridge University Press, 1984.

Bruneau, Thomas. *The Church in Brazil: The Politics of Religion.* Austin: University of Texas Press, 1982.

———. *The Political Transformation of the Brazilian Catholic Church.* London: Cambridge University Press, 1974.

Bussmann, Claus. *Who Do You Say? Jesus Christ in Latin American Theology.* Trans. Robert R. Barr. Maryknoll, N.Y.: Orbis, 1985.

Congar, Yves M.-J., O.P. *A History of Theology.* Trans. Hunter Guthrie, S.J. New York: Doubleday, 1968.

Cook, Guillermo. *The Expectations of the Poor: Latin American Base Communities in Protestant Perspective.* Maryknoll, N.Y.: Orbis, 1985.

Davis, Georgene Webber. *The Inquisition at Albi, 1299-1300.* New York: Octagon, 1974.

De Kadt, Emmanuel. *Catholic Radicals in Brazil.* London: Oxford University Press, 1970.

Della Cava, Ralph. *Miracle at Joaseiro.* New York: Columbia University Press, 1970.

Dorr, Donal. *Option for the Poor.* Maryknoll, N.Y.: Orbis, 1983.

Echegaray, Hugo. *The Practice of Jesus.* Maryknoll, N.Y.: Orbis, 1980.

Geffré, Claude, and Jean-Pierre Jossua. *True and False Universality of Christianity.* Concilium 135. New York: Seabury, 1980.

Hebblethwaite, Peter. *John XXIII: Pope of the Council.* London: Chapman, 1984.

Holmes, Derek. *The Papacy in the Modern World.* New York: Crossroad, 1981.

Jesudasan, Ignatius, S.J. *A Gandhian Theology of Liberation.* Maryknoll, N.Y.: Orbis, 1984.

Kennedy, Eugene. *The Now and Future Church: The Psychology of Being an American Catholic.* New York: Doubleday, 1984.

Knitter, Paul. *No Other Name? A Critical Survey of Christian Attitudes Toward the World Religions.* Maryknoll, N.Y.: Orbis, 1985.

Latin American Episcopal Council (CELAM). *The Church in the Present-Day Transformation of Latin America in the Light of the*

Council. Vol. 2: *Conclusions* (Medellín Documents). Bogotá, Colombia: General Secretariat of CELAM, 1970.

Levine, Daniel. *Religion and Politics in Latin America: The Catholic Church in Venezuela and Colombia*. Princeton: Princeton University Press, 1981.

Lumen Gentium. In *Vatican Council II: Conciliar and Post Conciliar Documents*. Ed. A. Flannery, O.P. Dublin, 1975.

MacDonald, Charles. *Church and World in the Plan of God: Aspects of History and Eschatology in the Thought of Père Yves Congar*. Frankfurt am Main: Peter Lang, 1982.

Nichols, Peter. *The Pope's Divisions*. New York: Penguin, 1981.

Novak, Michael. *Will It Liberate? Questions About Liberation Theology*. Mahwah, N.J.: Paulist, 1987.

Nunez C., Emilio A. *Liberation Theology*. Trans. Paul Sywulka. Chicago: Moody Press, 1985.

O'Meara, Thomas F. *Romantic Idealism and Roman Catholicism: Schelling and the Theologians*. Notre Dame: University of Notre Dame Press, 1982.

Richard, Pablo, et al. *The Idols of Death and the God of Life*. Maryknoll, N.Y.: Orbis, 1983.

Sacred Congregation for the Doctrine of the Faith. *Instruction on Certain Aspects of the "Theology of Liberation."* Boston: Daughters of St. Paul, 1985.

Schall, James V., S.J. *Distinctiveness of Christianity*. San Francisco: Ignatius, 1982.

Schoof, T. M. *A Survey of Catholic Theology 1800–1970*. Glen Rock, N.J.: Paulist Newman, 1970.

Schuon, Frithjof. *The Transcendent Unity of Religions*. Revised ed. Wheaton, Ill.: Theosophical Publishing House, 1984.

Schüssler Fiorenza, Francis. *Foundational Theology: Jesus and the Church*. New York: Crossroad, 1984.

Segundo, Juan Luis. *The Historical Jesus of the Synoptics*. Jesus of Nazareth Yesterday and Today, vol. 2. Maryknoll, N.Y.: Orbis, 1985.

———. *Theology and the Church: A Response to Cardinal Ratzinger and a Warning to the Whole Church*. (Appendix includes "Instruction on Certain Aspects of the 'Theology of Liberation.'") Trans. J. W. Dierksmeier. Minneapolis: Seabury, 1985.

Sobrino, Jon. *The True Church and the Poor*. Maryknoll, N.Y.: Orbis, 1986.

Sylvest, Edwin E., Jr. *Motifs of Franciscian Mission Theory in Sixteenth-Century New Spain Province of the Holy Gospel*. Washington, D.C.: Academy of American Franciscan History, 1975.

van Buren, Paul. *A Theology of the Jewish-Christian Reality.* Vols. 1 and 2. New York: Seabury, 1980.

The Worker Priests: A Collective Document. London: Routledge and Kegan Paul, 1954.

Books in Other Languages

Arce, Sergio, and Oden Marichal. *Evangelización y política.* Matanzas, Cuba: Centro de Información Ecuménica "Augusto Cotto," 1981.

Azzi, Riolando. *O catolicismo popular no Brasil: Aspectos históricos.* Petrópolis: Vozes, 1978.

Balthasar, Hans Urs von. *Kennt uns Jesus, Kennen Wir Ihn?* Freiburg im Breisgau: Herder, 1980.

Chenu, M.-D. *La Parole de Dieu II: L'Évangile dans le temps.* Paris: Editions du Cerf, 1964.

Deelen, Gottfried. *Kirche auf dem Weg zum Volke Soziologische Betrachtungen über Kirchliche Basisgameinden in Brasiler.* Mittingen: Brasielgoukunde, 1980.

Defois, Gerard, et al. *Le pouvoir dans l'Eglise: Analyse institutionnelle historique et théologique de la practique contemporain.* Paris: Editions du Cerf, 1973.

Duque, José. *La tradición protestante en la teología latinoamericana.* San José, Costa Rica: Departamento Ecuménico de Investigaciones, 1983.

Dussel, E., et al. *Tensões entre Igrejas ricas e pobres.* Concilium 164. Petrópolis: Vozes, 1981.

Fermet, A., and R. Marle. *Théologies d'aujourd'hui: J. Robinson, J. Ratzinger, H. Cox, H. Zahrnt, J. Moltmann.* Paris: Centurion, 1973.

Ferraro, Benedito. *A significação política e teológica da morte de Jesus a luz do Novo Testamento.* Petrópolis: Vozes, 1977.

Hartmann, Gunter. *Christliche Basisgruppen und ihre Praxis Erfahrungen im Nordosten Brasiliens.* Munich: Kaiser, 1980.

Henrich, Franz, ed. *Zwei Plädoyers: Hans Urs von Balthasar – Joseph Ratzinger.* Munich: Kösel, 1971.

Libanio, J. B. *As grandes rupturas socio-culturais e eclesiais: Sua incidência sobre a vida religiosa.* Petrópolis: Vozes, 1981.

Magaña, Alvaro Quiroz. *Eclesiología en la teología de la liberación.* Salamanca: Sígueme, 1983.

Pourraz, Robert. *La force des pauvres communautés chrétiennes au Brasil.* Paris: Editions du Cerf, 1981.

Ribeiro de Oliveira, Pedro. *Religião e dominação de classe Genêse: Estructura e função do catolicismo romanizado no Brasil.* Petrópolis: Vozes, 1985.

Rolim, Francisco Cantaxo. *Religião e classes populares.* Petrópolis: Vozes, 1980.

Segundo, Juan Luis. *Masas y minorías en la dialéctica divina de la liberación.* Buenos Aires: Aurora, 1973.

Articles in English

Cullen, Robert, et al. "Priests and Politics." *Newsweek,* April 14, 1986, pp. 44–50.

Dionne, E. J., Jr. "Joy and Doubt on Pope's Plan to Visit Synagogue." *New York Times,* March 20, 1986.

————. "The Pope's Guardian of Orthodoxy." *New York Times Magazine,* November 24, 1985, pp. 40ff.

————. "Pope Using Theme of Liberationists to Blunt Their Movement." *International Herald Tribune,* April 5–6, 1986.

"Doctrinal Congregation Criticizes Brazilian Theologian's Book." *Origins.* NC Documentary Service, vol. 14, no. 42, April 4, 1985.

Duffy, Eamon. "Urbi, but not Orbi . . . the Cardinal, the Church and the World." *New Blackfriars,* vol. 66, June 1985, pp. 272–278.

Dussel, Enrique. "Theologies of the 'Periphery' and the 'Center': Encounter or Confrontation." In Claude Geffré et al., eds., *Different Theologies, Common Responsibility: Babel or Pentecost?* Concilium 171. Edinburgh: T. & T. Clark, 1984.

Geffré, Claude, O.P. "Desacralization and the Spiritual Life." In *Spirituality in the Secular City.* Concilium 19. New York: Paulist, 1966.

Goldman, Ari. "Cardinal's Remarks on Jews Questioned." *New York Times,* November 18, 1987.

Hennessey, James, S.J. "Leo XIII's Thomistic Revival: A Political and Philosophical Event." *Journal of Religion,* Supplement, "Celebrating the Medieval Heritage: A Colloquy on the Thought of Aquinas and Bonaventure," vol. 58, 1978, p. S185.

Lash, Nicholas. "Catholic Theology and the Crisis of Classicism." *New Blackfriars,* vol. 66, June 1985, pp. 279–87.

Moynihan, Robert. "New Vatican document to stress a preferential love for poor, but will also urge Reconciliation," *National Catholic Register,* March 23, 1986.

————. "The Boff Brothers." *National Catholic Register,* June 21, 1987.

O'Leary, Joseph S. "Partners for Dialogue." *Inter-Religio,* Newsletter no. 8, Fall 1985, published by Nanzen Institute, Nagoyer, Japan.

Mignone, Fernando. "Ratzinger: This Time an Ovation." *National Catholic Register,* April 27, 1986.

Rahner, Karl. "Reflections on the Problems Involved in Devising a Short Formula of the Faith." In *Theological Investigations XI.* London: Darton, Longman & Todd, 1974.

———. "Towards a Fundamental Theological Interpretation of Vatican II," *Theological Studies,* vol. 40, no. 4, December 1979, pp. 716–727.

Ribeiro de Oliveira, Pedro. "The Romanization of Catholicism and Agrarian Capitalism in Brazil." *Social Compass,* vol. 26, nos. 2–3, 1979, pp. 309–329.

"Rio Refers Book to Rome, Brazilians Split." *National Catholic Register,* June 21, 1987.

Robinson, Paschal. "Bonaventure." *Catholic Encyclopedia,* vol. 2, p. 648. New York: Eniul Press, 1907.

Ruh, Ulrich. "The Conclusions of the Council of the Catholic Church and Faith." *Universitas,* 28/1, 1986, p. 11ff.

Shiraishi, Takash. "A 'Ritual' Revolution." *Look Japan,* vol. 32, no. 363, June 10, 1986, p. 28.

Steinfels, Peter. Review of *The Ratzinger Report.* In *America,* November 30, 1985, p. 388.

Woodward, Kenneth, et al. "Church in Crisis." *Newsweek,* December 1985, pp. 66ff.

Articles in Other Languages

"Arquidiocese do Rio examina novo livro de Boff, affirma d. Eugenio." *Folha de São Paulo,* February 17, 1987.

Bourdieu, Pierre. "Genèse et structure du champ religieux." *Revue Française de Sociologie,* 12:295–334.

Cadeñas, José. "Sobre fe y política." *Servir,* año 20, no. 108, 1984, p. 625.

Casaldáliga, Pedro. "Benedición de São Francisco para Frey Leonardo Boff." *Tempo e Presença,* no. 196, June 1985, p. 9.

Míguez Bonino, José. "¿Fue el Metodismo un movimiento liberador?" and "Justificación, sanctificación y plentitud." In José Duque, *La tradición protestante en la teología latinoamericana.* San José, Costa Rica: Departamento Ecuménico de Investicaciones, 1983.

"Outra vez na mira." *Veja,* June 17, 1987, pp. 60ff.

Perin, Orivaldo. "Novo livro de Boff ja esta quase condenado em Roma." *Jornal do Brasil,* May 17, 1987.

"Sie Sprechen miteinander." *Christ in der Gegenwart,* August 18, 1985, p. 1.

"Theologen gegen marxistische Analyse." *Frankfurter Allgemeine Zeitung,* August 2, 1985.

Index